The Librarian's Skillbook

51 Essential Career Skills for Information Professionals

Deborah Hunt and David Grossman

info@librarianskillbook.com
www.librarianskillbook.com

The Librarian's Skillbook:
51 Essential Career Skills for Information Professionals
by Deborah Hunt and David Grossman

Printed in the United States of America
First Printing, 2013
ISBN-10: 0989513319
ISBN-13: 978-0989513319

The Librarian's Skillbook
info@librarianskillbook.com
www.librarianskillbook.com

Ordering Information: Special discounts are available on quantity purchases by corporations, associations, colleges and universities and others. For details, contact the publisher at
info@librarianskillbook.com

This book is dedicated to David Richardson Peck, for his ever present support and sense of humor, and in memory of Karen J. Switt, who loved the library profession and taught so many the value of the skills presented in this book.

CONTENTS

ACKNOWLEDGMENTS

This book would not have been possible without the assistance of our amazing interns: Kim Hayden, Bonnie Hiller Fullerton, Kathryn Olson, and Jennifer Pickens. It takes a village (or a few outstanding interns) to write and publish a book.

We'd also like to thank all the librarians, students, and information professionals who have attended our Expand Your Career Potential workshops and webinars and encouraged us to put our workshop materials into print so they could have them easily at hand and so others could also benefit from them.

FOREWORD

You're holding a rarity. This book is a roadmap to your future as an information professional. The unspoken theme of this work is that "transformational librarianship" is the goal. What do we need to do to make ourselves essential, valuable, and hirable so we can make the difference we want to see in the world? If you find yourself frustrated, confused, or adrift at this point in your career, try the ideas outlined here.

I am honored to have read an advance copy of *The Librarian's Skillbook: 51 Essential Career Skills for Information Professionals*. What Deb and David have done here is to identify 51 highly useful skills that one learns through the *practice* of librarianship — that *cannot* be learned fully in any standard, formal educational experience, but must be acquired, based on our foundation of education and experiences, through a professional commitment to learning and the daily practice of librarianship. Indeed, they deliver a perspective informed by experience and wrapped in wit, wisdom, and practical advice. Regardless of the stage of your career, there is much to be learned here and the paths they identify are the right ones to focus on. There are 51 skill sets explored here. Each skill is described and positioned for its importance. Each has been informed by their personal experience and true-to-life stories. And each comes with further readings for you to explore and learn more.

This is more than a book that gets read alone. It is a roadmap, a plan, for you to follow to develop over your career and engage with the world of our field. It matters little if you're new to the information field or have dozens of years of experience. In the "practice" of librarianship we are all continuous learners and we all must adapt to changes and grow as professionals, managers, and leaders.

Technical or technological skills have always been important elements for long-term career success, but growing your soft skills — such as management, interpersonal relations, listening and influencing skills, and empathy — can make the difference between a competent professional and a great leader. You could choose to see the structure of this book as a personal learning plan for this year. It's really about your vision for yourself and the world and engaging with your passion to evolve, explore, and learn.

Take one week to construct your plan. Then select a different skill each week for the remaining 51 weeks in the year and focus on that skill. More importantly, don't just read and absorb — practice! Try out new skills. Learn a new technology. Adapt these skills to your challenges at work, job hunting, or describing your value to others. Don't set a goal to be an expert, but learn enough to understand and frame the opportunities presented by each skill. Work at your own speed but keep to a schedule. Add each skill to a regular day of the week in your calendar and keep a diary — in writing or on a personal blog journal — and then keep your commitment to yourself. Practice!

As David and Deb note, you're not trying to dive deep into each skill, but you're trying to understand each one and their frameworks to learn how they might apply to your personal, professional, or work situation. I promise, over time you'll grow, imperceptibly at first, but within months you'll be a better professional and better prepared to meet the challenges of the future as they arrive.

One of the challenges of being an information professional is that our field encompasses such a wide range of problems, solutions, and abilities. We are often loath to represent ourselves as "experts" in the fear that we might be overselling ourselves. That said, we do have a significantly greater "expertise" and insight in the information space since we sit at the confluence of content, technology, user experience, and professional service. That is a rare combination that we bring to the strategic discussions in our organizations as they struggle to position information and new technologies to the issues and decisions that need to be addressed. It also puts greater pressure on us as information professionals to develop ourselves as leaders and professionals. We need to particularly invest in those soft skills that buy us opportunities to influence others. This is an exciting time for us as practicing information professionals as the emerging information and knowledge-based economic ecosystem evolves for corporations, institutions, and society.

Deb and David conclude with six sure-fire strategies for career success. There are no magic beans here! What is required is simplicity itself — just a commitment to learn, practice, and make progress. You are your own best asset and every investment you make in yourself never goes for naught. I have known David and Deb for many years and admire them as friends and information professionals. As part of a community of information professionals who are committed to making a difference with their lives, the wisdom and plan outlined in this book provide an excellent start. Go. Engage. Develop.

Stephen Abram, MLS
Librarian and consultant with Lighthouse Partners and
Dysart & Jones, and creator of Stephen's Lighthouse blog

HUNT AND GROSSMAN

INTRODUCTION

WELCOME TO THE LIBRARIAN'S SKILLBOOK:
51 ESSENTIAL CAREER SKILLS FOR INFORMATION PROFESSIONALS

David and Deb's careers have taken some interesting detours, but we have never been without work. Why? Because we have continued learning and honing or adding skills to our toolbox that have allowed us to move between the library world and parallel worlds that don't always involve the "library" word.

The Librarian's Skillbook evolved from our Expand Your Career Potential workshops to help librarians and information professionals be more successful and advance their careers, both inside and outside the library world.

We started our workshops and wrote this book because:

- We see our colleagues struggling and wanting to change but not always knowing how

- We see vast career opportunities for librarians and information professionals
- We want to share our experiences and observations on best practices in career development
- We want to provide hope, inspiration, and a road map to expanding careers

In this book we will offer many tips and practical advice on how to move your career forward and acquire the vital skills necessary to improve your employment situation and future job prospects. It's all about skills. Having the right skills is the primary key to success for any career expansion or advancement. We will be discussing the many skills we see as the most critical, most sought after, most in demand for librarians and information professionals. Then we will provide you with a number of proven strategies or tactics that are useful for acquiring new skills that you cannot acquire in your current job or situation.

CHAPTER 1

WHY SKILLS ARE SO IMPORTANT

Having the right skills is essential to career expansion and success. We often hear about the skills we need to acquire but not why we should acquire them. This book will empower you to take control of your career and compensation.

> *"LIS skills are good currency, but only for those with the flexibility and insight to exploit the opportunities." —Stephen Abram, Dysart & Jones*

Stephen reminds us that our education and experience are just the jumping-off points for a successful career.

> *"Hiring managers assume someone with an MLIS degree has learned the requisite library skills. What differentiates job candidates are the other skills managers want." —Jill Hurst-Wahl, Associate Professor, Syracuse University School of Information Studies*

Jill is saying that the library/information skills that are most important to all of us are actually less important than we might think to most hiring managers in contrast to other non–library specific skills. This is because most hiring managers assume that we already possess all those standard library skills. They see all librarian job candidates on an equal playing field when it comes to the core library skills we are taught in library school.

For hiring managers, what differentiates some job applicants from the rest of the pack and what is most important to them are actually skills that are outside the realm of the standard library and reference skills we possess. These "outside" skills include business, interpersonal, and other skills that are not normally taught in library schools and iSchools.

According to Jill, the way to gain an advantage over other job candidates is to develop a proficiency in a skill that most other librarians may not have. In today's world, that might mean developing excellent writing or project management skills or a specific technical skill that only a minority of librarians are likely to possess, such as digitizing or creating databases.

This is radical thinking for most of us — that our library skills are just a prerequisite and that our chances of landing a job over the competition may hinge on our competency in skills outside the library realm and our ability to convince a hiring manager that you possess those other skills.

No one expects you to be an expert in all of the skills in this book. You need to know enough so that you can talk intelligently about these skills, and know where to go to acquire more learning to get up to speed. This can include continuing education (MOOCs or massive open online courses, association professional development workshops, webinars, reading) and volunteering in an information organization (or outside of one) to get the needed skills or strengthen current ones.

CHAPTER 2

THE TRANSFERABILITY OF SKILLS

What is your expertise and how do you articulate that to present and potential employers or clients?

In an ever-changing job market, it is important to acquire, strengthen, and express the skills we have developed that will take us to any area of librarianship, knowledge management, and the parallel universes where our skills are needed and valued.

Each of us has different strengths, skills, and interests. However, as libraries and their services evolve, we must change, too. While we may need core skills in traditional areas of library expertise, such as reference and collection development, we must move beyond those and add technology, business, management, interpersonal, attitude, and other tangible and intangible skills. Willingness to change is most important, for without it, we cannot move forward.

Transferable skills are ones we've acquired through jobs, volunteering, hobbies, and other life experiences that we can use as we move into new areas of our career. They are invaluable as we experience layoffs, are newly graduated, want to move up or out of our current job, or are reentering the workforce. These are the skills we've developed in one part of our life that are transferable to another. They empower us to break into a career area where we may not have any direct skills or experience.

CHAPTER 3

INTRODUCING THE 51 HOTTEST SKILLS
FOR LIBRARIANS AND INFORMATION PROFESSIONALS

"From the neatly defined roles reflected in library school courses of the mid-70s to the thousands of job titles collected in the SLA's recent salary survey, we librarians or information professionals definitely aren't what we once were. If we play our KM or 'knowledge engineer' cards right, there are very few areas in any organization in which we won't have significant contributions to make." (Colvin, 2009)

As library budgets and financial resources continue along a precarious path, there is an entire universe out there with numerous job opportunities and adequate funding. These opportunities are in organizations where our library skills (and the ones outlined in this book) can take us, if we can strengthen our skill set, recognize transferable skills, and add to the skills we already possess. These are the 51 hottest skills necessary to succeed and thrive in the library and information world and beyond.

This book describes what we believe are the most important, sought after skills that are in the greatest demand now and into the future. We not only describe the skills, but also provide tips to acquire the skills, and further readings. Some skills also have a definition, as well as a "This Skill in Action" example, to share how Deb, David, and our colleagues have used a skill in a real job situation.

As we mentioned earlier, no one expects you to be an expert in all the skills in this book. You need to know enough so that you can talk and act intelligently and know where to go to get more learning to get up to speed. Choose skills that will stretch you professionally and personally and some that seem easier. By mixing and matching the ones you choose, you'll acquire the greatest edge over your competition.

Which world do you want to live and work in?

The Traditional Librarian's World	-OR-	The Universe of Expanded Career Opportunities

CHAPTER 4

Computer and Technical Skills
You Need to Expand Your Career Potential

Every job today requires a level of comfort and expertise with computer and technical skills. Libraries are no exception. We may not be tweeting continually, but we must feel comfortable with skills ranging from document management (very similar to organizing library materials) to social networking and taxonomy creation. Most librarians will be surprised to learn they are already using many of these skills on a daily basis, but are referring to them with terminology we use in the library world. For example, metadata is the same principal as MARC fields, but you'll likely use Dublin Core fields rather than MARC field tags.

Here are 15 of the hottest computer and technical skills to get you on your way. Start with a few that seem most comfortable to you, and expand from there. Remember, you don't need to master them all, but do become familiar with what each one means and how it works for organizing knowledge and making it findable.

Skill #1: Digitization

> *"Digitization holds great promise for scholars and librarians alike. If projects are conducted properly, resources will be better preserved, and scholars will be able to discover and access these materials more easily than in the past." (McCraw, 2008)*

Description

Many describe digitization as "the hottest ticket in town" today — even for public and academic libraries. New technology has made digitization extremely inexpensive. Scanners are now affordable for anyone and digitizing vast collections of documents or images is now within the reach of even the smallest library, business, or organization.

When David arrived in his current position just seven years ago, creating a digital archive for the city of Mill Valley, California, the state-of-the-art scanner he purchased to digitize vintage photographs and other historic documents cost $3,000. Recently, as his department and the digitization project grew, David purchased three more scanners. Every staff workstation in his library now has its own scanner and he paid just $80 each for them. The quality is as good as, if not better than, the $3,000 scanner, and the scanning software out of the box is much easier to use.

With digitization costs dropping so dramatically, all kinds of organizations can now afford to digitize collections that were not possible or viable to be digitized just a short time ago. Additionally, programs like Photoshop and Acrobat Professional make it easy to enhance and reformat digitized documents and images.

Special collections being digitized by libraries, archives, historical societies, museums, and many other organizations and businesses include:

- Photographs
- Maps
- Audio/video tapes and films
- Handwritten letters
- Research papers
- Contracts and property deeds
- Meeting minutes
- Government or legal documents and briefings
- Laboratory notebooks
  ...and so much more

This has created an entirely new employment opportunity for librarians and information professionals or anyone with skill or experience digitizing a collection. Many organizations are searching for someone to manage or implement their digitization project or for additional personnel to assist in a digitization project already in progress.

This Skill in Action

David started his career working in the corporate library sector when online databases were brand new and then spent more than two decades on the vendor side, building online databases and retrieval systems for publishers, airlines, and library vendors. During that time, David never once thought that his online and electronic database/software experience would lead him into a job with a public library, but the growing affordability of digitization has created new high-tech jobs in every segment of the library and information world.

When David applied for his current job as the History Room librarian for the Mill Valley Public Library, he thought it was a long shot, since he lacked both the public library experience and history background. But it was his prior knowledge and experience with digitization and building databases that made David the ideal candidate to lead a town into the 21st century by converting its paper archive into a series of online databases using the latest digitization technology. That new technology improves access to the collection through online searching and makes it accessible to the world 24 hours a day, seven days a week through the library's website.

Instead of finding his resume beneath the pile of applicants with relevant experience from public libraries and historical societies, David's resume instantly floated to the top of the heap because of his experience digitizing maps for Rand McNally and creating online retrieval systems that allow consumers to book travel or manage their frequent traveler accounts on the internet.

Yes, David lacked the local historical knowledge and public library or archival experience, but no competing candidate with public library, history, or archival experience had any knowledge or experience with digitization, and the skills he had developed in his previous position were eminently transferable to this new environment. In the final analysis, it didn't much matter what David had digitized in his previous jobs — just the fact that he had digitization experience made him very valuable to his new employer.

At this point, although much of the world's knowledge has already been digitized, there is much more that still needs to be done and someone needs to manage those digital databases once they've been created. If you can acquire some digitization skills or experience, it may open a whole new world of interesting job opportunities that you may not have previously considered.

Tips to Acquire This Skill

Digitization is one of those skills that is probably best learned by doing. Find an organization or business that is already working on a digitization project and ask if it would be possible to volunteer as an apprentice to work on that digitization project.

If you can't find an organization already working on a digitization project, find one that ought to be digitizing its records or archives and offer to lead that project as a volunteer if they're willing to spend around $100 for a scanner that could be connected to any personal computer within the organization.

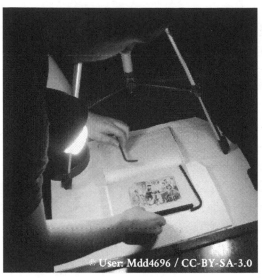

Even churches, schools, and civic organizations are good candidates for a volunteer-led project to digitize their records. You might also offer to digitize any publications they create, such as high school yearbooks, if those are not already accessible to the students and alumni in a digital format.

If you absolutely cannot find an organization willing to bring you on as a volunteer, consider purchasing your own scanner and digitizing a collection of whatever interests you most. Even a personal digitization project could help land a future job if you create a product that can be shown to a potential employer.

Further reading

1. Besser, H. (2003). *Introduction to imaging* (Rev. ed.). Los Angeles, CA: Getty Research Institute.
2. Landis, W. E. & Chandler, R. L. (Eds.). (2006). *Archives and the digital library*. Binghamton, NY: Haworth Information Press.
3. McCraw, E. (2008). Libraries and digitization: The state we're in. Retrieved from http://www.elizabethmccraw.com/projects.html

Skill #2: Electronic Indexing

Definition

Indexing, in the strictest sense, generally means assigning fields like title, author, or subject headings to a collection of articles, records, or other documents, so those documents or records can be organized, arranged, or sorted in alphabetical or numerical order and made searchable. Electronic or digital indexing is indexing performed in an electronic environment or using database software to create and house a database of indexed records.

Description

Digitization, discussed in the previous section, is a wonderful tool and skill to acquire, but most often, just digitizing a document or other item is not enough to unlock the potential that digitization can offer in creating an online database or electronic library. Digital documents or other items usually must be organized and indexed to make them fully accessible.

Indexing is all about:

- Describing content
- Developing hierarchical schemes
- Working with keywords, authority files, or controlled vocabulary lists
- Deciding what fields to use
- Deciding what goes into each field
- Formatting each field correctly for data entry
- And standardizing the format of the data being entered in each field

As librarians and information professionals, many of us already possess these skills or have experience in indexing. With electronic indexing, you may actually need to set up each field differently within a database system or software for it to properly accept the type and format of the data to be entered in that field.

Depending on the situation, you may need to apply an existing or standard electronic indexing scheme or develop a completely new and unique scheme applicable to a specific collection. Becoming familiar with some commonly used standard indexing schemes may come in handy, but simply developing the skill or acquiring the experience of electronic indexing, or even indexing in general, could be a critical skill for career advancement.

© Avaragado / CC BY 2.0

Tips to Acquire This Skill

If you can't find a paid position that would teach you indexing on the job, look for a small, nonprofit organization to develop your indexing skill. With digitization costs declining so rapidly, organizations that may be too small or lack the budget to hire an experienced indexer may be delighted to find a volunteer to index their records or other internal documents. This could include civic and religious organizations, as well as clubs or other nonprofit organizations. Starting in a small organization could give you the experience of taking an electronic indexing project from beginning to end with a simple database.

Further Reading

1. The American Society for Indexing,
   http://www.asindexing.org/
2. The National Information Standards Organization,
   http://www.niso.org/home/

3. Pitti, D. V. & Duff, W. (Eds.). 2002. *Encoded archival description on the internet*. Binghamton, NY: Haworth Information Press.
4. Santamaria, D. A. (2013). *Trends in archives practice module 3: Designing descriptive and access systems*. Chicago, IL: Society of American Archivists.
5. Schaefer, S. & Bunde, J. M. (2013). *Trends in archives practice module 1: Standards for archival description*. Chicago, IL: Society of American Archivists.

Skill #3: Digital Archiving

Definition

An archive is an accumulation of historical records preserved for historical purposes. Archives usually contain unique, primary source documents and other materials that do not exist elsewhere. Archived materials include rare books, manuscripts, personal papers, letters, organizational records, legal documents, photographs, films, posters, and memorabilia. A digital archive is an electronic archive most often created by the digitization of records or other documents from a paper archive.

Description

Digital archiving is a skill that often goes hand in hand with digitization and electronic indexing. While any collection of documents or other records can be digitized and indexed, digital archiving also includes all of the tasks centered around organizing and maintaining a digital archive.

The affordability of digitization by almost any organization has opened up a whole new world of opportunities in digital archiving that were never possible or feasible previously. Most organizations or businesses have records that date all the way back to the beginning of that organization. Until recently, these records have most often languished in boxes in a closet or the basement of that organization. Now, many organizations are looking to digitize those organizational or corporate archives, either as a way to provide better access to those records or to assure continued preservation into the future.

Beyond the digitization and preservation components of electronic archiving, there are also often the aspects of organizing and managing the physical paper archives. Fortunately, for librarians and information professionals, these parts of electronic archiving bear many similarities to traditional library work.

Although archivists have their own language, there are so many commonalities between libraries and archives that many graduate library programs also offer an archival track.

As electronic archiving continues to expand, the popularity of these archival tracks is growing. The good news for those who already possess a library science degree or who have been working in libraries for much of their careers is that they are already familiar with many of the principles that would also apply to archiving. Additionally, many archives are really a hybrid combination of library and archives, so having that library background will be extremely useful in those situations.

All a librarian or information professional needs to do to become an archivist is to learn those principles and practices of archiving that are not common to the library world. One area that can help is to become familiar with archival standards, such as Describing Archives: A Content Standard (DACS) or Encoded Archival Description (EAD) (see Further Reading on the next page for more information). DACS is a set of rules for describing archives, personal papers, and manuscript collections that can be applied to most archival collections. EAD goes beyond DACS to include the capability to describe a record's structural or encoding requirements and the actual verbiage to be used.

To broaden the scope of possibilities and employment opportunities, librarians and information professionals ought to consider learning enough about digital archiving to make them a viable candidate for many archival jobs.

Tips to Acquire This Skill

As with electronic indexing described in Skill #2, librarians and information professionals might want to find an organization without a budget to hire a professional archivist and to take over the creation of a digital archive from scratch. The smaller the organization, the less likely they will need to use standard archival practices and the more likely that existing traditional library skills may be applicable for much of the archiving work. Additionally, the more an archive must also double as a library, the more qualified an existing librarian or information professional will be in performing that job.

To bolster archiving skills, a librarian or information professional might want to check with different library schools about the possibility of taking some archival coursework. With so many library schools now offering online distance-learning programs, information professionals are no longer limited to schools within their immediate geographic area.

Additionally, a librarian or information professional might want to check with the Society of American Archivists or the Northeast Document Conservation Center (see Further Reading, below) to see what types of training those organizations can provide.

Further Reading

1. Daines, J. G. (2013). *Trends in archives practice module 2: Processing digital records and manuscripts*. Chicago, IL: Society of American Archivists.
2. Encoded Archival Description, http://www.loc.gov/ead/
3. Landis, W. E. & Chandler, R. L. (Eds.). (2006). *Archives and the digital library*. Binghamton, NY: Haworth Information Press.
4. Northeast Document Conservation Center, http://www.nedcc.org/
5. Society of American Archivists, http://www2.archivists.org/
6. Society of American Archivists. Describing archives: A content standard. Chicago, IL: Society of American Archivists. Retrieved from http://ow.ly/lIsI0
7. Sproull, R. F. & Eisenberg, J. (Eds.) (2005). *Building an electronic records archive at the National Archives and Records Administration: Recommendations for a long-term strategy*. Washington, DC: National Academies Press.

Skill #4: Metadata Creation and Management

> *"It has become more important than ever that... information professionals... understand the critical roles of different types of metadata in ensuring accessible, authoritative, interoperable, saleable, and preservable cultural heritage information and record-keeping systems." (Gilliland, 2008)*

Definition

The word "metadata" means "data about data." In the library world, metadata are the information used to search for and describe an object, record, or other item. Objects could include books, magazine articles, photographs, video files, maps, MP3 music files, etc. Typical metadata elements include title, author/creator, subjects, keywords, publisher, etc.

Description

Many librarians and information professionals may not know that they are already conversant with metadata, because they don't realize that they've been using it throughout their career. Metadata has been around since the earliest days of library catalogs and archives. The Dewey Decimal Classification system, along with the author, title, subject headings, and even an abstract included on the old library catalog cards are examples of metadata in common use. All of the metadata on a catalog card describes the book or other object in the collection and the Dewey and subject headings also convey the location of the book and the alphanumeric schema used for physical location arrangement. For example, physics books will always be located in the "530" section and history books on Peru will always be found in the "985" section.

Just like the indexing and archiving skills described in the previous sections, familiarity with metadata must often accompany the digitization skill. As information becomes increasingly digital and available online, the importance of metadata and metadata standards is also on the rise. Both the indexer and the searcher must select the same concept or relevant documents for records to be successfully retrieved.

To facilitate the effective use of metadata, many standards have evolved, and becoming familiar with some of the more popular ones could greatly increase any librarian or information professional's opportunities for career growth.

Most librarians and information professionals are already familiar with the MARC (Machine-Readable Cataloging) standard developed by the Library of Congress. Two more recently developed metadata standards are extremely noteworthy for librarians and information professionals interested in career advancement in this area. Those standards are Dublin Core and METS (Metadata Encoding and Transmission Standard).

The Dublin Core metadata standard is a set of vocabulary terms that can describe a wide range of objects, such as photographic images, audio/video, artworks, artifacts, web pages, etc. Dublin Core currently contains 22 distinct data elements:

1) Title	9) Publisher	17) Provenance
2) Subject	10) Contributor	18) Rights Holder
3) Description	11) Rights	19) Instructional
4) Type	12) Date	Method
5) Source	13) Format	20) Accrual Method
6) Relation	14) Identifier	21) Accrual
7) Coverage	15) Language	Periodicity
8) Creator	16) Audience	22) Accrual Policy

We see an increasing number of job descriptions seeking candidates who are conversant with Dublin Core or METS and you might be called upon to administer a collection using either of these metadata standards in a future job.

Whether you are using one of the widely accepted metadata standards or developing your own custom metadata scheme that will be unique to your collection, using a controlled vocabulary system of metadata can greatly increase access to your collection versus simply asking researchers to search using text strings, as the general public is accustomed to doing with Google and other internet search engines.

Metadata schemes can be hierarchical or linear, like Dublin Core. They can also use authority or controlled vocabulary lists or allow free text in certain fields. In any case, it's all about the best way to describe content in a collection.

This Skill in Action

In David's history library/archive, he elected to develop his own metadata standard after assessing the contents of his library's historic collections of photographs, maps, oral histories, and other documents and objects. This decision was made because David felt his collection was unique to the community and that it would not need to interface with any other collection that might be using a more universal metadata standard. But before David arrived at this conclusion, he spent considerable time examining Dublin Core and METS, which helped greatly in developing the standard for the Lucretia Little History Room. So even if you are faced with a similar situation where developing a new, homegrown metadata scheme seems like the best option, it is still advantageous to review some of the more popular metadata standards.

In developing a homegrown metadata scheme for the Lucretia Little History Room, David and his staff first looked at the contents of the various collections and listed all of the data elements necessary to accurately describe the objects in each collection. These became the various data elements or fields. For example, some of the fields used to describe the library's photograph collection include a title, a description, a date or date range, the photographer's name if known, the photo donor's name, the size and color of the photo, the names of people, places, or events depicted in the photo, as well as a list of descriptive words or phrases that would be useful in retrieving that photo. David's team also performed this exercise for the library's maps, oral histories, newspaper articles, books, and other collections.

Next, they decided which information should go into each field and whether that information could be standardized into a list of commonly used words or phrases to describe each object or whether the field should allow free text data entry. Then David's team decided on the formats to be used for the data entered in each field.

Tips for Acquiring This Skill

Although there are many proactive steps librarians and information professionals can take to learn more about metadata, many of us already have substantial knowledge in this area from our current or previous jobs or library school training. To become more conversant with metadata, it could be useful to read more information about the various popular metadata standards in use today. Librarians and information professionals should also contact their colleagues in other libraries or archives and conduct informational interviews to see how they might be using metadata.

Finally, while it may be difficult for a novice to find a paying job involving the development or management of a metadata scheme, numerous volunteer opportunities abound. Librarians and information professionals interested in acquiring this skill should ask their colleagues if they need any volunteer help to assist with metadata data entry or collection management, or find an organization that has a collection that could benefit from the application of a metadata scheme even if that organization doesn't currently have a librarian or a budget to make this happen for them.

Further Reading

1. Digital Library Federation. (2010). METS: Primer and reference manual. Retrieved from http://www.loc.gov/standards/mets/METSPrimerRevised.pdf
2. Dublin Core, http://dublincore.org/metadata-basics/
3. Gilliland, A. J. (2008). *Setting the stage. Introduction to metadata* (p. 1). Los Angeles: Getty Research Institute.
4. METS, http://www.loc.gov/standards/mets/
5. Miller, S. J. (2011). *Metadata for digital collection: A how-to-do-it manual.* Atlanta, GA: Neal-Schuman Publishers, 2011.
6. National Information Standards Organization. (2004). *Understanding metadata.* Bethesda, MD: NISO Press. Retrieved from http://www.niso.org/publications/press/UnderstandingMetadata.pdf
7. Smiraglia, R. (2012). *Metadata: A cataloger's primer.* Binghamton, NY: Haworth Information Press.

Skill #5: Taxonomy Construction and Management

> *"The taxonomist works with different user communities as well as developers and helps bridge the gap between what users and experts know and what is needed to build a useful application. A classy taxonomist has a well-rounded set of skills that can work with development teams and user organizations to build intelligent systems."* (Taxonomy Blog, 2010)

Definition

A taxonomy is a system to organize or categorize knowledge composed of the terms used to describe a file or resource. Taxonomies can be of several types, listed here from least to most complex:

- **Term list**: simple list of terms, usually alphabetical
- **Synonym ring**: controlled vocabulary
- **Authority file**: controlled vocabulary with synonyms, often used for proper names
- **Hierarchical taxonomy**: can have many levels, sublevels, and subheadings
- **Thesaurus**: consists of broader, narrower, and related terms
- **Ontology**: represents knowledge as a set of concepts within a domain, and the relationships between pairs of concepts

Description

A good taxonomy takes into account the elements of a group and its subgroups that are mutually exclusive, but taken together, include all possibilities. Taxonomies help us create efficiency in our everyday lives as well as in the lives of organizations. Common taxonomies include the Library of Congress Subject Headings, MeSH, DTIC, and Carl Linnaeus' classification of all living things, the Systema Naturae. Linnaeus' system is a good example of a taxonomy as it goes from the general to the more specific. For example, a sunflower is classified thus:

> **Common job titles**
> - Information Architect
> - Ontologist
> - Taxonomist
> - Taxonomy Consultant
> - Taxonomy Editor

- **Kingdom**: Plantae
- **Subkingdom**: Tracheobionta
- **Superdivision**: Spermatophyta
- **Phylum**: Magnoliophyta
- **Class**: Magnoliopsida
- **Subclass**: Asteridae
- **Order**: Asterales
- **Family**: Asteraceae
- **Genus**: Helianthus L.
- **Species**: annous

There are ready-built taxonomies out there, such as the ones named above, but often you may build one from scratch depending on the collection you are describing. There is taxonomy software that can be used to develop and deploy a taxonomy, but some organizations just use a spreadsheet or generic database.

This Skill in Action

A defense contractor designs and sells high-powered rifle scopes, software, accessories, cases, mounts, and more. These products are specific to this company and a custom hierarchical taxonomy was created to describe them. Excel was used to create the taxonomy. This was a challenging project that took a couple of months of creation, testing, and tweaking till it worked satisfactorily with the document management system being used. It also had to be scalable for new products that would be developed by the company in the future.

Tips to Acquire This Skill

There are many taxonomy websites to get you up to speed quickly (see Further Reading below for resource websites). SLA.org has a Taxonomy Division that offers workshops, tips, and a community of sharing and expertise. LinkedIn has the Taxonomy Community of Practice, which has great discussions going on.

Further Reading

1. Hedden, H. (2010). *The accidental taxonomist*. Medford, NJ: Information Today.
2. Hedden, H. (2010). Taxonomy made easy: An introduction to taxonomies for the accidental taxonomist. Earley & Associates. Retrieved from http://www.hedden-information.com/Taxonomy%20Made%20Easy.pdf
3. LinkedIn Taxonomy Community of Practice, http://ow.ly/je2hA
4. SLA Taxonomy Division, taxonomy.sla.org
5. Taxonomy Community of Practice, http://taxocop.wikispaces.com/TaxoTools

Skill #6: Document Management (DM)

Definition

Document management (DM) is the computerized management of electronic and paper-based documents.

Description

Strategic knowledge is every organization's most valuable asset. The volume of data and information within an organization is accelerating at a rapid pace. Efficient organization and findability of information can result in enhanced customer service, improved internal communication, better informed decision making, increased productivity, and greater ROI (return on investment), while reducing staff frustration.

Document management (DM) provides the foundation to turn corporate assets into shared knowledge by providing a central information source accessible to knowledge workers.

DM systems have been around for over 30 years, originally developed as a system to enable the paperless office. Early DM systems were limited in complexity to scanning and electronically retrieving paper documents. These early file and find systems were simply electronic filing cabinets.

More recent technological advances have revolutionized DM. DM systems capture almost any type of document or asset in almost any format (e.g., paper, digital, XML, email, etc.). DM enables dramatic gains in efficiency and productivity by improving the way organizations categorize and manage business documents, information, and processes.

Many DM systems are integrated into MS Office and Windows Explorer, so assets appear as a virtual disk drive.

Very useful features of a DM system usually include:
- Simple and advanced search options

- Viewing documents in a hierarchical structure (to facilitate drilling down to content)
- Asset check-in and check-out to prevent simultaneous changes
- Version control, which preserves old versions and includes a user log of all changes, time stamps, and the identity of the individual who initiated those changes
- Secured web access from anywhere with a remote connection, either via the cloud or via virtual protocol network (VPN) to an organization's internal server
- Permissions/security control indicating who can view, edit, or create each asset type
- Synchronization when moving between offline and online mode
- Support of multiple document formats, including MS Office documents, PDF files, CAD drawings, images, paper document scans, and more

A major DM capability is workflow. Workflow is defined as an IT technology that uses electronic systems to manage and monitor business processes. It allows the flow of work between individuals and departments to be defined and tracked.

DM is no longer a file and find system. It has evolved to include tracking the process of distributing documents and monitoring and controlling work. This is sometimes called e-processing or a workflow for e-business, which extends beyond an organization to its partners, customers, and suppliers. DM is a must have for any for-profit or nonprofit organization to remain competitive.

This Skill in Action

Several years ago, Deb was engaged by an environmental engineering firm to organize and automate its library. As she met with staff, Deb realized their real challenge was finding the firm's internally created assets so they could be reused and repurposed for reference and future work. Deb proposed organizing, increasing findability of, and improving access to this internal information to be comparable to the organization and access to externally created content in the library.

Stakeholders immediately realized this was what they really needed and Deb initiated an information audit to create the business requirements criteria. Based on the criteria, Deb identified a software solution that would allow for both indexing of library and internally created content. Deb recommended hiring cataloging librarians who were enthusiastic and capable of completing the project. Those catalogers recognized that their cataloging skills were transferrable to the 21st century and that they could use those skills to organize both the internal and external content.

Tips to Acquire This Skill

Information professionals and librarians already know how to organize information for findability. We are familiar with metadata and taxonomies (though we may call them something else, such as MARC, Dublin Core, or subject headings).

Many DM software systems offer free training and trial downloads so you can learn how to use them and evaluate their fit for your organization. Hundreds of DM vendors, trial versions, and demo information may be accessed at Capterra's website (see Further Reading on the next page). You can use filters to limit your software search results to a more manageable number.

Offer to lead or participate in a DM initiative within your organization to learn how to use the software and how to make valuable documents and assets findable. If an employment opportunity is not readily available, consider implementing a DM project for friends or family. You might also consider crafting an internship or volunteering to perform DM for a nonprofit organization if no other viable alternatives exist.

Further Reading

1. Association for Information and Image Management (AIIM). What is document management? Retrieved from http://www.aiim.org/What-is-Document-Management
2. Capterra's list of document management software programs, http://ow.ly/cyAnG
3. Nason, D. (2011). Document, content, knowledge: Part 1, document. Retrieved from http://EzineArticles.com/6415852
4. Turk, B. (2011). Document management: An overview. Retrieved from http://ow.ly/lluFL

Skill #7: Enterprise Content Management (ECM)

> *"ECM promotes pervasive, rich and interactive information management for an organization. It is a mature concept which has evolved to match information technology and business needs." (Cameron, 2011)*

Definition

The Association for Information and Image Management (AIIM) defines enterprise content management (ECM) as the strategies, methods, and tools used to capture, manage, store, preserve, and deliver content and documents related to organizational processes. ECM tools and strategies allow the management of an organization's unstructured information, wherever that information exists.

Description

ECM tools and strategies allow the management of an organization's unstructured information wherever that information exists. ECM adds economic value to an organization's assets. It is more than document management, which generally looks at a document or resource as a whole. ECM allows for templatized documents, parts of which can be linked to other document pieces to create new content on the fly.

Technology plays a key role in ECM, but is not the business decision driver. Before one begins to consider technology or software solutions, one must review organizational functions, including:

- Document management with expanded capabilities of lifecycle management
- Electronic records management/DAM
- Workflow
- Collaboration
- Web content management
- Security, both in terms of documents and who has permissions to view, edit, and delete
- Search and browsing for content

Tips to Acquire This Skill

There are hundreds of ECM software vendors who teach free webinars on ECM. Yes, they will be touting their product, but you will nonetheless learn from the webinars. You can also access AIIM.org to check out free webinars as well as their ECM certification courses.

> **Common job titles**
> - Team lead, records management
> - Senior records management specialist
> - EC, ERM, and governance officer

Further Reading

1. AIIM.org ECM certification courses, www.aiim.org/Training/ECM-Enterprise-Content-Management-Course
2. AIIM.org Research and Publications, http://www.aiim.org/Research-and-Publications
3. Cameron, S. A. (2011). *Enterprise content management: A business and technical guide.* Swindon, UK: BCS. Retrieved from http://ow.ly/llE40
4. LInkedIn EnterprIse Content Management Network, http://ow.ly/jbJyO

Skill #8: Knowledge Management (KM)

Definition

> *"Knowledge management is the deliberate and systematic coordination of an organization's people, technology, processes, and organizational structure in order to add value through reuse and innovation. This coordination is achieved through creating, sharing, and applying knowledge as well as through feeding the valuable lessons learned and best practices into corporate memory in order to foster continued organizational learning." (Dalkir, 2011)*

Description

So many organizations are information rich, but insight poor. There is an old saying: "Information is power." But that is only true if we can find the right information. To turn information into strategic knowledge, organizations must make better use of their internal and external information resources and expertise. Sharing and learning must be top of mind and practice for an organization and it is essential to have buy-in and participation from senior management to be successful.

Effective KM makes relevant information readily available so that users can make timely valid decisions. KM is a practice rather than a product. It is an environment that fosters knowledge

sharing among organizational staff. Sharing is the key word here as it benefits everyone in the organization. Following on sharing is learning and training, both informal (sharing something with a colleague on the spur of the moment) to more formal (in a workshop or webinar).

So far, we have not talked about technology. Yes, there are tools for harnessing tacit knowledge, but a KM program must first have goals and objectives, including a knowledge audit, staff dedicated to seeing a KM initiative through, buy-in from management, and goals and objectives in place. There are social tools and software available to make sharing easier, but someone needs to ensure that the foundation is in place to make a KM initiative successful and adopted throughout the organization.

Tips to Acquire This Skill

There are many KM/KS websites to get you up to speed quickly (see Further Reading on the next page for urls to the resources mentioned in this section). There are also formal programs, such as the one at Columbia

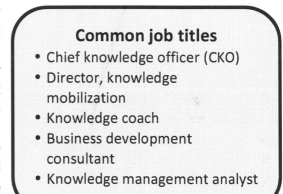

Common job titles
- Chief knowledge officer (CKO)
- Director, knowledge mobilization
- Knowledge coach
- Business development consultant
- Knowledge management analyst

University. SLA.org has a KM Division, which has lots of good information, and SLA's ClickU has an excellent series of KM courses leading to certification, which are taught by the guru of KM, Guy St. Clair. KM software vendors offer lots of information on their websites and free online demos and webinars. Look for opportunities to have your expertise recognized. Start small and then move to high-profile projects. Be proactive instead of reactive.

Further Reading

1. Australian River Restoration Center. (2010). Developing an information and knowledge strategy. Retrieved from http://ow.ly/iwbZb
2. Columbia University MS in Information and Knowledge Strategy program, http://ce.columbia.edu/Information-and-Knowledge-Strategy
3. Dalkir, K. (2011). *Knowledge management in theory and practice* (2nd ed.). Cambridge, MA: MIT Press.
4. Special Libraries Association (SLA) KM Division (members only), http://wiki.sla.org/display/SLAKM/
5. Journal of Knowledge Management. Emerald Group Publishing Limited. ISSN 1367-3270.
6. LinkedIn KM Jobs: Knowledge Management Career Board, Advice & Networking, http://ow.ly/jtCOM
7. LinkedIn Knowledge Management Group, http://ow.ly/jtCHM
8. LinkedIn Women in Knowledge Management, http://ow.ly/jtCWt
9. Special Libraries Association (SLA) ClickU, http://www.sla.org/learn/certificate-programs/cert_knowledge_mgmt/

Skill #9: Knowledge Services (KS)

> *"Knowledge Services is putting knowledge management to work — it's the practical side of KM." —Guy St Clair.*

> *"At its most successful, Knowledge Services is about establishing social communities, about creating the social infrastructure, a foundation of trust, and a collaborative environment in which all stakeholders contribute to the successful achievement of the parent organization's mission. It is the ideal tool for enabling specialized research libraries to support the larger organization in achieving its objective." (St. Clair, 2003)*

Definition

Knowledge services (KS) brings together information management, KM, and strategic learning to deliver business value from organizational knowledge.

Description

An organization's success is based upon it being able to tap into its largest asset: the knowledge of its employees, clients, and business partners. Intellectual capital, the stuff in people's heads, is a competitive asset, and much of it walks out the door when an employee leaves an organization. Capturing that tacit knowledge is the key to KS and an organization's ability to thrive.

Tips to Acquire This Skill

Just as with KM, there are many KS websites to get you up to speed quickly. There are also formal programs such as the one at Columbia University (see Further Reading below). Great online and in-person webinars are online and often are free. Look for opportunities to have your expertise recognized. Start small and then move to high profile projects. Be proactive instead of reactive.

Common job titles
- Information specialist
- Chief information officer (CIO)
- Director, knowledge services
- Strategic knowledge capabilities director
- Global knowledge exchange director

Further Reading

1. Columbia University MS in Information and Knowledge Strategy program, http://ce.columbia.edu/Information-and-Knowledge-Strategy
2. LinkedIn KM/Knowledge Services Group, http://ow.ly/jtCp4
3. Clair, G. S., et al. Towards world-class knowledge services: Emerging trends in specialized research libraries part two: The customer perspective. SMR International. Retrieved from http://ow.ly/lIEC5
4. St. Clair, G. & Stanley, D. (2011). Building the knowledge culture: The knowledge services effect. SMR International. Retrieved from http://ow.ly/lr1ZT

Skill #10: Records Management (RM/RIM)

Definition

Records management (RM) is defined as the systematic control of records throughout their lifecycle. It is also known as records and information management (RIM) and electronic records management (ERM), depending on whether the format of what is being managed is paper or digital.

Description

Just as libraries organize information in the form of books, journals, e-resources, and more, and have policies for collection development, acquisitions processes, and weeding or disposition, organizations create records every day. These record types are often dependent on the type of organization, be it corporate, a government entity, or academic institution. But, many organizations have record types in common, such as emails, contracts, human resources files, financial records, and much more.

Why Records Management?

Records management has been around since organizations began creating and keeping records of what they do. The formats may have changed over the years from paper-based to digital, but RM is still valuable as records are the information assets that define, drive, and record the history and work of the organization. More importantly, effective RM can directly affect an organization's ability to compete in the marketplace, comply with regulations, and recover from disaster.

What are records? They are the stuff of an organization's history and work.

They come in many formats, including:
- Paper
- Email and their attachments
- Instant messages
- Extranet and intranet content
- Content on e-devices, such as computers, laptops, tablets, smartphones, thumb drives, and shared drives
- Social media such as LinkedIn and Facebook

RM Governance

ARMA International has published Generally Accepted Recordkeeping Principles (GARP) (see Further Reading at the end of this skill) which offers much useful information for assessing how an organization is effectively organizing its records. It provides both a standard of conduct for governing information and metrics by which to judge that conduct. GARP describes and measures fundamental attributes of information governance. It is the handbook for RM/RIM governance.

What Tools Are Needed for RM?

There are many products and services out there, including:
- Classification and taxonomy
- Compliance
- Consulting services
- Content/document management applications
- Data conversion
- Digital/video preservation
- Disaster recovery
- Document capture
- Document destruction
- Records storage
- Equipment and supplies
- RIM software

These product offerings can make RM/RIM more productive, and some also offer document management and enterprise content management capabilities. ARMA's Buyer's Guide is a good starting point to see which companies offer which services and software (see Further Reading).

This Skill in Action

A civil engineering firm had thousands of paper blueprints, landscape design documents, and highway schematics, all rolled up and stored one on top of another in boxes on the floor, stacked against walls, and all over tables in the print room and in staff offices. Some were ordered by project number or year of creation and others not at all. The challenge was to retain the rolled format, but make the documents

**"Cut off" your files—
before they cut *you* off!**

For more information, contact your records officer or the
National Archives' Agency Services Division 301-713-6677.

National Archives and Records Administration 1992

easily and quickly findable. (Most of these records were old enough that no digital version existed.) All other project records for the firm were already organized by project number, with some stored in print and others digitally. The solution to organize these rolls by project number was an easy one, but how to physically store them was more challenging. A database of existing documents was created, including the corresponding project number, and special shelving and labeling were designed to make it possible to find documents.

Tips to Acquire This Skill

Information professionals and librarians already know how to organize information for findability and many are already familiar with cataloging, collection development, weeding, and disposition of resources. Some aspects of RM/RIM differentiate it from library work, including:

- Legal and regulatory aspects
- Data Conversion
- Software
- Storage of paper and digital records

There are many ways to acquire RM/RIM skills. In your own organization, check to see if RM/RIM is in place. If not, offer to lead an initiative. Do your homework, presenting why it is important for the organization to comply with legal and regulatory requirements while preserving vital records. If this isn't possible, find or create an internship or volunteer opportunity to learn firsthand. Many RM vendors offer free webinars and white papers. They are listed in ARMA's Buyer's Guide (see Further Reading, below).

ARMA and Archives Association of British Columbia both offer free and fee-based online courses, podcasts, publications, and certification. Many library and iSchools offer online and in-person classes, as well. DMOZ Open Directory Project has a long list of RM associations (see Further Reading, below), which may also offer courses.

Further Reading

1. Archives Association of British Columbia. (2012). The AABC archivist's toolkit. Retrieved from http://aabc.ca/resources/archivists-toolkit/
2. Archives Association of British Columbia. (1999). A manual for small archives. Retrieved from http://aabc.ca/media/6069/manualforsmallarchives.pdf
3. ARMA Buyer's Guide, http://archive.arma.org/buyersguide/indexw2.cfm
4. DMOZ Open Directory Project list of RM associations, http://www.dmoz.org/Reference/Archives/Records_Management/Associations/
5. Generally Accepted Recordkeeping Principles (GARP), http://www.arma.org/r2/generally-accepted-br-recordkeeping-principles
6. Richardson, B. (2012). *Records management for dummies*. Hoboken, NJ: John Wiley & Sons.

Skill #11: Digital Asset Management (DAM)

Definition

Digital asset management (DAM) consists of management tasks and decisions surrounding the ingestion, annotation, cataloging, storage, retrieval, and distribution of digital assets. A subfield of DAM is media asset management (MAM), which includes digital photos, animations, videos, and music.

Description

Many organizations first think of software or technology when considering DAM, but it is really a combination of the people, processes, assets, and technology involved. DAM content is continually growing and changing. Content that is tagged with metadata and connected to a taxonomy relevant to the organization's culture and vocabulary is findable, valuable content.

Some key features of DAM systems include:

- Relationships and grouping among assets
- Asset upload and download
- Permissions and security controls on who has access, viewing, and editing rights to assets
- Workflow
- Version control
- Creation of asset collections
- On-the-fly editing

This Skill in Action

The Exploratorium undertook a DAM project as the museum approached its 40th anniversary, when management and staff recognized content was becoming unmanageable and being deleted, lost, or thrown out. There were print files as well as digital shared folders and files on hard-drives, with no file name standards, no taxonomy, nor anything much in the way of organization for retrieval and duplicate detection. Two librarians and one publications department staff member were chosen to lead the project, with additional help from a system administrator.

Why were librarians chosen to lead this project? These two librarians were involved in many projects from fostering international online educator communities and partnering with other museums on nanoscience, youth initiatives, and much more. Their job title was senior information specialist and the museum recognized the valuable skills and connections they brought to projects.

The librarians first performed a needs assessment. Based on those results, they created the business requirements criteria for selecting a software solution and then went through the process of RFIs (requests for information) and reviewing them, finally settling on a software solution. They built out a metadata schema and taxonomy and gathered materials, reformatting from obsolete formats (such as Hi8 tape), scanning and OCRing (optical character recognition), and much more to render the assets readable and findable.

Tips to Acquire This Skill

There are many DAM software vendors that have lots of information and free webinars, as well as LinkedIn groups to get you up to speed quickly — see Further Reading below for resource urls. If you tweet, follow #damgeek on Twitter.

Further Reading

1. Cliffe, N. & Yurkovic, M. (2011). Digital asset management road map: The secrets of a successful dam implementation. Retrieved from http://damroadmap.com/

2. DAM LinkedIn group, http://ow.ly/jdP3y
3. DAM Pros, http://ow.ly/jdPgv
4. Diamond, D. (2012). DAM survival guide. CreateSpace. http://damsurvivalguide.com/
5. Elguindi, A. C. & Schmidt, K. (2012). *Electronic resource management: Practical perspectives in a new technical services model.* Cambridge, UK: Chandos Publishing.
6. Harvey, R. (2010). *Digital curation: A how-to-do-it manual for librarians.* Atlanta, GA: Neal- Schuman Publishers.

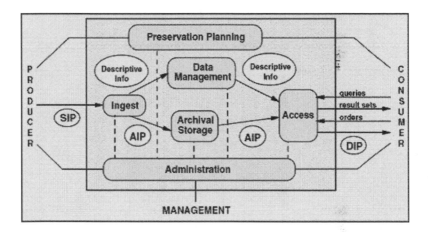

Skill #12: Developing Finding Aids/ Pathfinders

"Now that finding aids are often posted on the internet, their level of descriptive content, visual design, and layout are more important than ever, because many researchers are likely to refer to them without first consulting the archivist." (Morris & Rose, 2010)

Definition

A "pathfinder" may be defined as one who discovers a new course or way. In library terminology, a pathfinder refers to a print or electronic guide that can describe the sources available on a particular subject. In contrast, a finding aid is a document containing detailed information about a specific collection of papers, records, or other documents within an archive or library.

Description

While there is a distinct difference between pathfinders and finding aids, researchers use both tools to assist them in research. As more collections are digitized and put online, making them infinitely more accessible for public access, the need for creating both good finding aids and pathfinders becomes increasingly important.

Pathfinders may include print or electronic sources of information within a single library or in multiple libraries, as well as sources available through the internet or other online sources.

The content of a finding aid may differ depending on the type of material it describes. Usually, a finding aid includes a list or description of the contents as well as a description of the scope of a collection. This could include biographical or historical information related to that collection and any restrictions on use of or access to those materials. Finding aids may also include lists of subject headings or other controlled vocabulary.

Most finding aids use the Encoded Archival Description (EAD) format, which is a set of widely recognized international standards maintained by the Library of Congress and the Society of American Archivists.

This Skill in Action

In the local history library/archive in the public library where David works, there is a growing need for both pathfinders and finding aids and David has brought in library science and archival students and mid-career librarian interns to create a series of these very useful documents.

David's interns have created many subject-specific pathfinders detailing sources within his local history library, other libraries in the area, and online sources. These pathfinders include topics such as the railroad that ran through town a century ago, nearby Muir Woods National Monument, or the Native American tribes that populated the region before European settlers arrived, as well as pathfinders on how to find information about local businesses, homes, or streets. In contrast, finding aids in development focus on specific collections, such as the oral history collection, the map collection, or a collection of historic postcards from the area.

Tips to Acquire This Skill

If you've never created a pathfinder or a finding aid previously, the first step may be to look around you and see if there is a topic or a collection in your current environment that would benefit from the creation of one or more of these guides. Fortunately, there are many excellent examples of good pathfinders and finding aids easily accessible on the internet. (See Further Reading on the next page for links to examples.) If you are developing a finding aid, try to create one using the DACS or EAD standards described in this section and discussed previously in "Digital Archiving" (Skill #3). Many employers are seeking someone who is familiar with EAD or DACS.

If you cannot develop a pathfinder or finding aid at your current job, look around for volunteer opportunities, like the kind David is offering in his library/archive. Also consider organizations that may not have a library, but have a collection of something that needs to be organized and described.

Further Reading

1. EAD format, loc.gov/ead/
2. Finding aid example, http://besser.tsoa.nyu.edu/impact/f95/Site_visits/findingaid.html
3. Finding aids, http://www.loc.gov/rr/ead/
4. Mann, A. C. How to make a good library pathfinder. Retrieved from http://amycmann.wordpress.com/practical-experience/continuing-staff-development/make-a-pathfinder/
5. Morris, S. L. & Rose, S. K. (2010) Invisible hands: Recognizing archivist' work to make records accessible. In A. E. Ramsey, W. B. Sharer, B. L'Eplattenier & L. Mastrangelo (Eds.), *Working in the Archives: Practical Research Methods for Rhetoric and Composition* (66). Carbondale, IL: Southern Illinois University Press.
6. Online Archive of California, http://www.oac.cdlib.org/
7. Pathfinders, http://www.ipl.org/div/pf/
8. Sample annotated finding aid, http://www2.archivists.org/usingarchives/appendix
9. Santamaria, D. A. (2013). *Trends in archives practice module 3: Designing descriptive and access systems*. Chicago, IL: Society of American Archivists.
10. Schaefer, S. & Bunde, J. M. (2013). *Trends in archives practice module 1: Standards for archival description*. Chicago, IL: Society of American Archivists.

Skill #13: Website Design

Definition

Website design means the planning, creation, and updating of websites. Website design also involves information architecture, website structure, user interface design, navigation structure, website layout, colors, fonts, and images. All these elements combined together form websites.

Description

Many of us may not be required to create a website from scratch, but knowing enough basic code to make updates and edits (especially when a text editor won't let you do exactly what you want to

© 1artlv / CC BY-ND 2.0

do) is a great skill to have. We may be responsible for overseeing and editing an extranet or intranet site in as simple a way as updating information on an ILS (integrated library system) homepage or creating a portal to internally created assets in our organization.

This Skill in Action

A few years ago, Deb's company, Information Edge (information-edge.com), needed a new look and website. Deb worked with a graphic artist and web designer to create her new site. (She just didn't have the time or skill set to build it herself.) Now she makes all the updates and additions to content herself, including new issues of her e-newsletter and blog. It is not a steep learning curve, yet challenging enough to keep Deb on her toes.

Tips to Acquire This Skill

There are many, many resources out there and a few are noted in the Further Reading section. If you want to play with website creation and design, Google Sites is a good sandbox where you can experiment. On the opposite end of the spectrum is Adobe Creative Suite, which includes Dreamweaver, a powerful but pricey web creation tool. In the middle is WordPress which Deb and David are using for this book's website (librarianskillbook.com). It is free, though there are premium upgrades and many, many templates, styles, and social connectors to get the word out about your site. There is also a lot of community around WordPress where you can ask questions and get answers.

Further Reading

1. Google Sites, http://sites.google.com/
2. HTML and CSS for Beginners MOOC, http://coursetalk.org/codecademy/html-css-for-beginners
3. Lynda.com (has 29 courses in HTML and 430 on website design)
4. Robbins, J. N. (2012). *Learning web design: A beginner's guide to HTML, CSS, JavaScript, and web graphics.* Sebastopol, CA: O'Reilly Media.
5. WordPress, http://wordpress.com/

Skill #14: Social Networking

"U.S. libraries of all types are turning more and more to social media... using a wide range of applications to connect with customers. Facebook and Twitter in particular have proven themselves as useful tools not only in publicizing the availability of online collections, but also in building trusted relationships with users." (2012 State of America's Libraries Report)

Definition

A social network allows you to connect with friends, family, and colleagues, and share photos, videos, and personal and professional information with either a select group of people or a broader network, depending on the settings you select.

Social networking isn't new, it's just that now we do much of it online. Think of your circle of family, friends, and colleagues. They make up your social network. Now, though, you can take it way beyond that by connecting with colleagues and others whom you may never meet in person.

Social networks like Facebook, LinkedIn, and Twitter are great ways of keeping in touch with friends and family around the world as well as making new connections with people based on similar interests or professions. There are many different social networks that you can join — all for free.

Description

What is your presence on LinkedIn, Twitter, and Facebook? What is your brand? You may think you do not have a brand, but if you are on social networking sites, you certainly do. Current and potential employers, clients, and others who wish to network will look at your presence and brand. What do you want them to see?

What is the best way to connect with others and which social network is best for you? That depends. Deb has both a Facebook and LinkedIn presence, but uses Facebook mostly for connecting with family and friends. LinkedIn is  her professional face where she connects with colleagues and friends in groups by posting updates and asking and answering questions. She also created a group called Career Sustainability (ow.ly/kV4NY) and invites you to join to ask and answer questions or even just lurk.

Deb tweets and retweets when she finds valuable knowledge to share, or is at a conference or other professional development event and wants to share with those not attending. It's easy to tweet and follow other tweets if you use a free app like Hootsuite or Tweetdeck.

Some information professionals use tweets and other social media to mine intelligence, from who works where or which company may be hiring in a particular area of expertise to who is tweeting about a new product offering.

This Skill in Action

Deb had a taxonomy question for a client project and was able to post to several LinkedIn digital asset and taxonomy groups as well as SLA and other listservs. She received valuable advice and was also able to summarize what she learned back to the groups she had queried. She has not met most of those who responded, but social networking made it possible to garner their expertise no matter their location or organization.

Tips to Acquire This Skill

If you don't have a LinkedIn profile, start one. LinkedIn and other social networking tools have great video and other help tools that make it easy to get started. Take advantage of those tutorials and get your profile online. If it's already there, make it a point to update it on a regular basis. Or, start with Facebook and see the fun you are missing. Once you are an online social networker, spend about 10 minutes a day updating and viewing content. It's a great investment for a very small amount of time.

Further Reading

1. *2012 State of America's Libraries Report.* American Libraries, 34. Retrieved from http://www.ala.org/news/sites/ala.org.news/files/content/Sta teofAmericasLibrariesReport2012Finalwithcover5.pdf
2. Facebook: Get started, https://www.facebook.com/help/467610326601639/
3. Hootsuite, http://hootsuite.com/
4. LinkedIn: Help, http://help.linkedin.com/
5. O'Neill, M. The complete guide to twitter. Retrieved from http://www.makeuseof.com/pages/download-guide-twitter
6. Tweetdeck, http://www.tweetdeck.com/

Skill #15: 21st Century Cataloging

> *"An online [cataloging] system makes it possible to streamline our library operations, to implement standards that ensure consistency in our cataloging and circulation, to make searching the... library resources easier for users, and to help our users become more self-sufficient." (Fong, 2012)*

Definition

21st century cataloging is original cataloging or creation of metadata used to describe unique, sometimes one-of-a-kind materials, that are often held by a single library so catalog records are not available through the Library of Congress (LC), OCLC, or anywhere else.

Description

For decades, many in the library world have predicted the demise of cataloging. With the proliferation of online union catalogs, and OCLC and LC opening their catalogs to any library, it seemed like original cataloging and catalogers at individual libraries were headed for obsolescence. Was there no longer a need to waste precious resources cataloging a book or other material that has already been cataloged by someone else? In this new era of automation, perhaps all libraries need do is download that catalog record from LC or OCLC to their OPAC and dispense with the laborious, often tedious task of original cataloging.

In many cases, the need for original cataloging may no longer be a necessity, but it would be a grave mistake to write off the art or science of cataloging completely just yet. While new technology has made cataloging of popular books and other widely available materials largely superfluous, that same new technology has also stimulated a growing need for original cataloging for many other materials. The proliferation of digitization, online databases, and on-demand, self-published works has created a whole new class of unique bibliographic resources not accessible through LC or OCLC, and therefore requires original cataloging by the owner or creator of those one-of-a-kind items.

As digitization and online database creation costs diminish, more organizations are digitizing collections of internal documents, drawings, video, audio, and more. The same is true of archival collections of photographs, letters and other historic documents. In many cases, only one library or organization may ever own these unique items. Therefore, that library must create its own original catalog record without assistance from the outside world.

As the need for original cataloging of popular materials declines, fewer library and information school students are taking cataloging classes. In fact, cataloging is no longer a requirement in many library and information school programs. This has produced a new generation of librarians who don't know how to catalog. Anyone with cataloging skills or experience has a distinct advantage here.

This Skill in Action

The Lucretia Little History Room where David works is a local history library/archive that is part of a 20-branch library consortium in Marin County, California. Like many other libraries, original cataloging within the Marin County branch libraries has become largely unnecessary as the catalog records for most public library purchases are uploaded from OCLC to the library system OPAC and catalogers at the individual libraries subsequently copy that record or add their library name to the county catalog record for that item.

In contrast, History Room staff and volunteers routinely conduct original research and create and self-publish new oral or video histories, photograph albums, scrapbooks of letters, and many other unique publications covering local history. There is no

OCLC or LC record for most History Room works because those items are one of a kind. Without relying on OCLC, the catalogers normally assigned to catalog History Room materials are not equipped to catalog the original, home-grown, historic materials.

The History Room is also constructing an online database composed of individual photographs, maps, oral/video histories, letters, and other unique items. As these items are digitized, History Room staff must catalog and add metadata to the online database software. Whether adding History Room self-published items to the county OPAC or entering the metadata into the database software for each unique, digitized item, 21st century cataloging is required to complete the task and any librarian without those skills is unable to adequately perform the required work.

Tips to Acquire This Skill

Identify a collection of unique materials at work or home that has never been cataloged, and catalog it. If this opportunity doesn't exist in your current work or home environment, try contacting an historical society, archives, museum, or public library in your area to see if they might have a need for original cataloging. Many organizations without a hiring budget deploy volunteers to help digitize and catalog historic collections and you may be able to join a project already in progress or get them started in creating a new database that would require original, 21st century cataloging. You can also acquire this skill by taking a cataloging class in a local library or information school or a paraprofessional certificate program.

Further Reading

1. Fong, C. (2012). From manual to online cataloging. *The New Librarian*. Retrieved from http://www.aallnet.org/main-menu/Publications/aall-ilta-white-paper/cataloging.pdf
2. Jones, B. M. (Ed.). (2003). Hidden collections, scholarly barriers: Creating access to unprocessed special collections

materials in North America's research libraries. *RBM: A Journal of Rare Books, Manuscripts, and Cultural Heritage*, 5(2), 88-105. Retrieved from http://rbm.acrl.org/content/5/2/88.full.pdf+html

3. Roe, K. D. (2005). *Arranging and describing archives and manuscripts*. Chicago, IL: Society of American Archivists.

4. Russell, B. M. (2004). Special collections cataloging at a crossroads: a survey of ARL libraries. *Journal of Academic Librarianship*, 30(4), 294-303. Retrieved from http://ow.ly/lIzlO

5. Sanchez, E. (Ed.) (2011). *Conversations with catalogers in the 21st century*. Santa Barbara, CA: ABC-CLIO.

6. Wakimoto, J. C. (2009). Scope of the library catalog in times of transition. *Cataloging & Classification Quarterly*, 47(5), 409-426.

© Trevor Owens

CHAPTER 5

Beyond Reference Skills
You Need to Expand Your Career Potential

We all most likely feel comfortable doing a reference interview and helping our customers find the information they need when they ask for it. However, we need to move beyond reference to provide knowledge and information that will directly contribute to the health and well-being of our organization or clients. We must continually be proactive, seeing needs that are not being met, anticipating where we can provide added value, and having the vision to be top of mind for our customers.

The following seven skills are really hot. Mastering and using them will lead to job security, more career opportunities, and the satisfaction that we contribute positively to the bottom line of the organization.

Skill #16: Strategic Knowledge/ Advantage

"Library and information services in corporations, schools, universities, and communities capture information about their users, circulation history, resources in the collection, and search patterns (Koenig, 1985). Unfortunately, few libraries have taken advantage of these data as a way to improve customer service, manage acquisition budgets, or influence strategic decision-making about uses of information in their organizations." (Nicholson & Stanton, 2003)

Definition

Strategic advantage involves communicating a greater perceived value to a target market than competitors can provide.

Description

Strategic knowledge/advantage can be achieved many ways, including by offering a better-quality product or service (such as power searching using a paid database rather than Google) or contributing positively to the bottom line by providing strategic knowledge that end users could not find on their own. Sustainable strategic advantage refers to maintaining a favorable position over the long term, which can help boost your image as well as your value and future contributions to the organization.

Strategic advantage results from matching core competencies to opportunities. We need to align with and analyze the mission and goals of our organization, users, and clients. Based on this analysis, we can make strategic decisions and then take action. This empowers us to deliver the strategic knowledge our users need to do their work and thrive. This is an essential skill we need both for our own sustainability and that of our organizations.

Tips to Acquire This Skill

© www.lumaxart.com / CC BY 2.0

Research the goals, mission, and strategic objectives of the organization using a SWOT analysis to find strengths, weaknesses, opportunities, and threats. Once you've done this, create a strategy to capitalize on opportunities with your target audience. Initiate conversations to find out where their pain points and challenges are. Then find a way to bring relief that will provide you with a strategic advantage and your target audience with strategic knowledge.

Further Reading

1. Genesys. (2013). Five ways to transform customer service into a strategic advantage. Retrieved from http://research.thewhir.com/content26992
2. Nicholson, S. & Stanton, J. (2003). Gaining strategic advantage through bibliomining: Data mining for management decisions in corporate, special, digital, and traditional libraries. In H. Nemati & C. Barko (Eds.), *Organizational data mining: Leveraging enterprise data resources for optimal performance* (247-262). Hershey, PA: Idea Group Publishing.
3. Smith, J. L. (2006). *Creating competitive advantage: Give customers a reason to choose you over your competitors.* New York, NY: Crown Business.

Skill #17: Results-Driven Problem Solving

> *"Minimize... risk by arming yourself with a thorough understanding of your customers and your competitors — and the day-to-day local issues that affect their decisions."* (Phelps, 2011)

Definition

Results-driven problem solving helps end users solve a problem and determine a course of action, instead of simply presenting the user with a number of options to choose from.

Description

There was a time when being a librarian often meant sitting at the reference desk waiting for users to approach you with a question. Those days are over. Users are increasingly going on the internet themselves, diverting potential business away from the reference desk and ultimately bypassing librarians altogether for quick and easy answers to many questions.

While end users generally lack the sophistication and skill of a librarian in online searching, most are quite capable of finding answers to basic questions with the self-service internet. This phenomenon has transformed the role of a librarian in most situations.

With the easiest questions and answers removed, librarians and information professionals need to establish their value by successfully handling the most difficult questions. In today's fast-paced world, it's no longer good enough to provide the requested information and walk away. The best librarians and information professionals always go one step beyond just providing information by focusing on results-driven problem solving.

In today's complex world, end users want to find someone who can provide the best solutions to their business, technical, and even personal problems. This presents a great challenge to librarians and information professionals.

How can librarians and information professionals become expert enough in the business of their end-user customers to be able to recommend solutions to their problems? To be successful in results-driven problem solving, librarians and information professionals must learn how to ask the right questions and strive to understand their end users' business and the environment they inhabit.

With results-driven problem solving, it's no longer a question of "Give me all the articles about making widgets." The question for today's librarians and information professionals is, "Please tell me how our company can make the best widgets on the market."

This Skill in Action

In a previous position, David worked for a major corporation that produced products for human consumption. One day, this company discovered it had a huge rodent problem in one of its production facilities. In the old days, David and his staff might have been called upon to perform an online search and produce a list of articles to give to the plant manager, but in most cases that will no longer suffice.

David's quest was to find a rodenticide as quickly as possible that could eradicate the rodent infestation without presenting a toxicity problem for the people working in the factory. The plant manager was obviously in a panic and didn't have time to sift through reams of paper and read a mountain of articles to try to determine a course of action; he wanted and expected David and his crew to not only perform the search, but to sift through all the results and make the decision — a vital decision that could spell success or disaster — and give that plant manager the name of a chemical or product that could do the job effectively. This is an example of results-driven problem solving.

The need and expectation for results-driven problem solving cuts across all types of libraries and impacts all aspects of the profession. Even in David's current part-time role as a reference librarian, the

public expects much more than a point in the right direction. While some people still ask the librarian to show them where the travel books about Sicily are, one phone caller asked David if he could tell her if it was possible to take a bus between Palermo and Syracuse. She wanted to know the bus schedules, the fares, and how she could purchase her ticket. In this role, David not only played reference librarian, but also took on the role of travel agent, tour guide, or concierge, providing a total solution for that library patron. That is results-driven problem solving in action.

In any environment, it's all about playing an essential role and providing a critical piece of the solution to a major problem faced by your organization or your customer.

Further Reading

1. Bates, M. E. (2011). Why insight matters. EContent. Retrieved from http://www.econtentmag.com/Articles/Column/Info-Pro/Why-Insight-Matters-75773.htm
2. Phelps, M. (2013). Ask the right questions to get the right answers: Effective market research requires preparation. Retrieved from http://www.cobizmag.com/articles/ask-the-right-questions-to-get-the-right-answers?

Skill #18: Provide "Value Add" Solutions

Definition

> *"Value add" is the enhancement added to a product or service before offering it to customers. Librarians and information professionals take a product or service that may be considered homogeneous and provide customers (or potential customers) with a feature or add-on that gives it a greater sense of value.*

Description

Adding value to any service or product we provide sets us apart from others in a good way. Making others look good by providing more than they expected is a win-win. This leads to improved customer perception and support. As others begin to see and experience the value we add to projects, research, and other areas of our organization, we are perceived as an asset rather than overhead. Adding value is a good brand to have, especially when it positively affects the bottom line.

This Skill in Action

When Deb worked in a museum, she started a weekly event she called Tech Tuesdays in the library. Library staff kept their ears to the ground to learn about what potential research, skills, and resources were needed by museum staff and members, often before they even realized they needed them. Deb and her staff used the Tech Tuesdays to teach (or recruited other museum staff to teach) skills such as tweeting, using library databases, and more. Soon, staff were coming to the library on days other than Tuesdays to eat lunch, read journals, or just hang out. The library became THE place for professional development and collaboration.

Tips to Acquire This Skill

Think of an experience you've had where someone provided a service or favor that went far beyond what you expected. How did that make you feel? Was it memorable or even remarkable? That is the kind of "value add" we want to provide that makes our services, expertise, and value memorable. Try it and you will be amazed at the customer loyalty that will follow.

Further Reading

1. Morin, P. (2012). The importance of differentiation and adding value. Retrieved from http://www.companyfounder.com/2012/01/the-importance-of-differentiation-and-adding-value/
2. Seath, I. (2008). Value add: How to quantify it. Retrieved from http://ianjseath.files.wordpress.com/2009/04/value-add.pdf

Skill #19: Research and Analysis

"No matter how much market research you do, how sophisticated your tools or how connected your network of experts, you won't find the answers to the questions that matter without a strategy... Whether you're doing research for yourself, your company or your clients, the best way to prepare your strategy is by asking the right questions right from the start... To get the right answers, you need to ask the right questions — and taking the time to get ready for research will drastically improve your results." (Phelps, 2013)

Definition

Research is a service most of us provide to our users. Analysis goes beyond the research by providing insight based on the information or knowledge discovered.

Description

Long gone are the days when we hand our end users a bibliographic list of search results. In order to add value, we must provide an analysis and synthesis of what we find and, if appropriate, make recommendations. This can take the form of a short one-page executive summary outlining the research done, an analysis of what was found, and recommendations for action. This empowers the customer and makes us invaluable.

Often, the customer will want more than the executive summary — the bibliographic list of sources found, abstracts if available, or even the full text of resources. Having a template already in place makes this easy to format and very readable for the customer. Including graphics in research deliverables is another way to add value, such as using charts to display data.

Tips to Acquire This Skill

You may already be doing analysis, but had not realized it. For example, every time you look for a restaurant using a service such as Yelp, you research the type of food you want to eat, the restaurant location, and more. Those are your search parameters or strategy. Once you get that list, you then do an analysis to figure out which works best for you based on budget, group size, parking, etc. Once you do the analysis, you can choose the best restaurant for your needs.

We can do the same type of analysis on research we do for our users. Don't wait to be asked; just include it. If you think you are too busy, then you need to focus on this value-added service and let others go. Your customers will definitely be impressed and your value will go up in the organization.

Further Reading

1. Kangiser, A. (2003). Delivering competitive intelligence visually. *Competitive Intelligence Magazine*, 6(5), 20-23. Retrieved from http://www.onlinebusinessresearch.com/CI%20Sep_Oct%2003%20Kangiser.pdf
2. Kassel, A. (2002). Value-added deliverables: Rungs on the info pro's ladder to success. *Searcher*, 10(10), 42-53. Retrieved from http://www.infotoday.com/searcher/nov02/kassel.htm
3. Microsoft Word Report Templates, http://office.microsoft.com/en-us/templates/results.aspx?qu=reports&av=zwd
4. Phelps, M. (2012). Visualization tools for turning information into insights. *Online*, 36(5), 14-19. Retrieved from http://www.infotoday.com/online/sep12/Phelps--Visualization-Tools-for-Turning-Information-Into-Insights.shtml

Skill #20: Competitive Intelligence (CI)

Definition

Competitive intelligence (CI) is the process of monitoring an organization's industry or market to identify (1) current and future competitors, (2) their current and announced activities or product releases, (3) how their actions will affect the organization, and (4) how to respond. CI uses legal and ethical means to gather and sift publicly available information.

Description

Competitive information supports a variety of competitive intelligence questions by providing in-depth background reviews, current snapshots, and early warning of changes in markets, technology, government regulations, consumer interests, and political environments.

In today's global economy, there is fierce competition for business. No longer is it enough just to do research, collect data and information, and present a list of articles and urls. We need to move beyond that to intelligence that will empower an organization to survive and even thrive. This is as true for Fortune 500 companies as it is for small business.

On the following page, you'll see a simple way to understand the difference between data, information, and intelligence.

Data, Information, and Intelligence

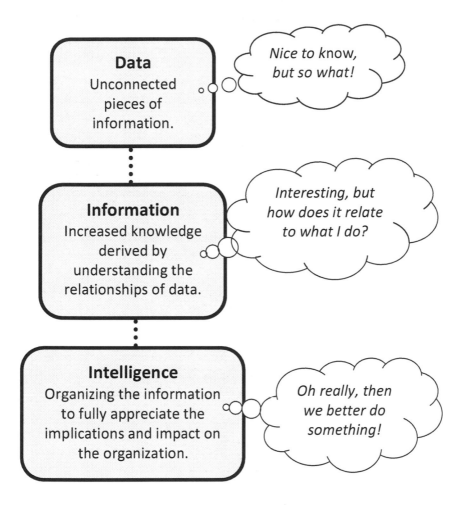

Most of us collect CI without even realizing it — we read professional publications, attend conferences or trade shows, and network and share information with colleagues both inside and outside our organizations. However, there are other aspects of CI that are necessary for an organization to benefit from it. One can scan public records, monitor the internet, and speak with customers, suppliers, industry experts, staff, academics, and other knowledgeable parties.

Here is the process for collecting CI:

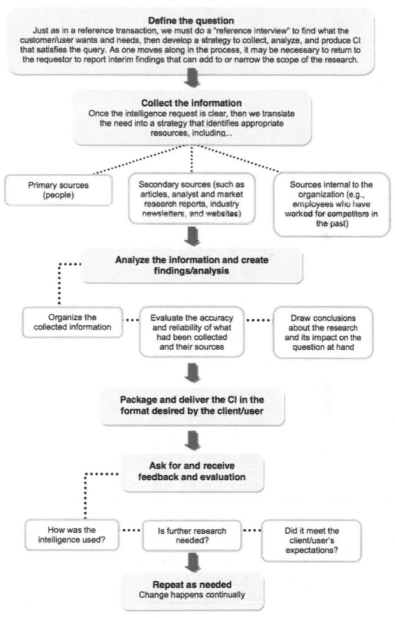

The CI collected should be actionable so the organization can move forward to remain competitive in its market or sphere. CI empowers our clients and users to know what the competition is up to. We must be top of mind for the "C suite" and our stakeholders to be the source of this intelligence.

This Skill in Action

A pharmaceutical client was considering adding a new heart medicine to its product line. This was a new area of medicine for the company and they wanted to see what the landscape was as far as who else might be considering developing and offering this type of drug. They already had a good idea of what their competitors were doing in their current line of products, but they needed intelligence to form a basis for whether this would be a logical and profitable drug to develop.

Using CI strategies, Deb initiated research to find what competitors were up to and which areas they were considering going into or had already invested in. Following the steps for a CI project above, Deb:

1. **Defined the question**: Were the client's competitors in the pharmaceutical industry planning to fund research to launch a drug that would treat this heart condition? As the research progressed and unexpected information came to light, Deb would communicate with her client about new intelligence and make recommendations for any adjustments to the research.

2. **Collected the information**

    a. *Primary sources*: Deb picked up the phone and talked to researchers at top university medical centers, leading cardiologists, and others who might have insights into what was coming down the drug pipeline from competitors.

    b. *Secondary sources*: Using pharmaceutical databases on Proquest Dialog, news resources on

Factiva, and the open web, Deb looked for press releases, articles, white papers, and analyst reports that might shed light on competitors' plans.

c. *Sources internal to the organization*: She talked to the client's employees who had formerly worked for competitors.

3. **Analyzed the information and created findings/analysis**
   a. Deb organized the collected information in a way that made it easy to compare conflicting intelligence and weed out what seemed irrelevant.
   b. Deb evaluated the accuracy and reliability of what had been collected to judge which intelligence was most reliable.
   c. Deb drew conclusions about the research for this project and included that intelligence in her report.

4. **Packaged and delivered the CI in the format desired by the client/user**
   a. Deb delivered, via email, the intelligence in the form of a report created in Word and Excel with a one-page executive summary. After the stakeholders had an opportunity to read the report, she had a live conference call with them to discuss the findings and next steps.

5. **Asked for and received feedback and evaluation**
   a. The client said the intelligence was spot on and decided to go ahead with the huge investment in developing the new drug.
   b. At that point, no further research was needed.
   c. The client confirmed that Deb's report met expectations.

6. **Repeated as needed**
   a. There was no follow-up research with this project.

Tips to Acquire This Skill

Information professionals and librarians already know how to tease from users the information and intelligence they are seeking and to utilize secondary research tools such as those on the open web and from database providers such as Proquest Dialog and PrivCo. Primary research is something many of us have done as well — we've picked up the phone, had a hallway conversation, or emailed someone who is knowledgeable in the area of intelligence we are seeking. LinkedIn also provides CI. One can search to see if a company has laid off lots of employees (search under people, then company name) and the organizations those employees have moved to.

Building on those skills, one must then hone the skill of filtering information, pulling out the nuggets of intelligence, and analyzing them. One can use Porter's Five Forces model or a SWOT analysis to identify strengths, weaknesses, opportunities, and threats. There are many tutorials online to learn how to use these tools.

Offer to lead or participate in a CI initiative within your organization to learn how to do this. If an employment opportunity is not readily available, consider a CI project on a subject or organization that interests you. Do you love Apple products? If so, use Apple as your CI subject. Interested in electric cars? Use that. You get the idea.

Further Reading

1. Competitive intelligence tools. (2012). Retrieved from http://aqute.com/s/Competitive-Intelligence-Tools.pptx
2. Porter's five forces: Assessing the balance of power in a business situation. Retrieved from http://www.mindtools.com/pages/article/newTMC_08.htm
3. Strategic and Competitive Intelligence Professionals (SCIP), http://www.scip.org/
4. SWOT Analysis: Discover new opportunities. Manage and eliminate threats. Retrieved from http://www.mindtools.com/pages/article/newTMC_05.htm

Skill #21: Thinking Outside the Box

> *"One of the crucial roles of info pros is to bring a distilled view of the external world into their organizations. Our responsibility is to ensure that we bring as rich and nuanced a view as we can, and that can involve bringing attention to the things that just don't look quite right. Who knows the impact that can have?" (Bates 2011)*

Description

Thinking outside the box is a concept we've all heard before. It's such a simple concept to grasp, yet often very difficult to put into practice consistently. Yet, it is this precise type of thinking that often drives so many innovations.

So what do we really mean by saying "thinking outside the box" and how can librarians and information professionals make this a reality every day? Thinking outside the box in the work environment means trying to think about things in different ways, but it also means continually asking yourself, "Is there anything we should be doing differently that we're not doing now?"

Those who are capable of thinking outside the box are also consistently focused on finding ways to improve processes or better perform existing tasks within their organization. Note here the use of the word "organization" rather than using the word "library." This is significant because to make a true impact with your out-of-the-box recommendations, you will want those ideas to affect the entire organization, not just your library.

Tips to Acquire This Skill

Unlike many of the computer and technical skills we've discussed in the previous sections, thinking outside the box is one of those more intangible skills that probably can't be taught, but comes naturally with practice. To acquire this skill, librarians and information professionals need to train themselves to ask every day, "Is there anything we should be doing differently that we're not doing now?"

This means continually questioning current standard practices and methods at your organization. And since you are trying to think outside the box for your entire company or organization, that means you need to proactively go out of your own department to learn how things are being done in other departments or areas of your organization. It means you need to  learn all you can about the entire organization, so you can make out-of-the-box recommendations that could impact the entire operation.

Another way to encourage out-of-the-box thinking is to challenge subordinates, peers, and supervisors to also think outside of the box. You may not come up with an out-of-the-box solution to every problem, but encouraging others to do the same will likely increase the chances that someone will propose an out-of-the-box solution that could solve that problem and you will have been the catalyst to make that happen.

Further Reading

1. Bates, M. E. (2011). Why insight matters. *EContent*. Retrieved from http://www.econtentmag.com/Articles/Column/Info-Pro/Why-Insight-Matters-75773.htm
2. Cox, D. (2013). *Creative thinking for dummies*. England: John Wiley & Sons Ltd.

3. De Bono, E. (1999). *Six thinking hats*. Boston: Back Bay Books.
4. Michalko, M. (2006). *Thinkertoys: A handbook of creative-thinking techniques* (2nd ed.). Berkeley, CA: Ten Speed Press.

Skill #22: Seeing the Big Picture

Description

Like "Thinking Outside the Box" (Skill #21), "Seeing the Big Picture" is another one of those intangible skills that probably comes most often with practice, experience, and a ubiquitous awareness of its significance. This is another skill that involves focusing on the entire organization rather than just your own library or department.

Organization presidents and chief executive officers are tasked with seeing the big picture and focusing completely on achieving organizational goals. A good chief executive always makes decisions that benefit the entire organization even if that comes at the expense of one or another department within the organization.

Another aspect of seeing the big picture is looking ahead into the long-term future rather than focusing solely on meeting immediate goals and objectives. Failure to look far into the future, and instead focusing solely on the next quarter or the current year, has put many companies in jeopardy. Seeing the big picture from a time perspective might mean sacrificing immediate revenue or profits to invest, creating better products or retooling to provide better services to customers or constituents over the long term.

Finally, seeing the big picture also implies not getting lost or bogged down in the details. This often means allocating the bulk of your time and energy to focus on the few areas that will have the most impact rather than trying to address everything at once. It can also mean avoiding the trap of seeking perfection in every little area at the expense of achieving the overall goal.

In the business world, many believe in the 80/20 rule. When used in a sales and customer environment, the 80/20 rule means that 80% of your business comes from 20% of your customers, while only 20% of your business comes from the other 80% of your customers. In this example, it is clear to see that any organization facing this situation ought to be spending the bulk of its time paying attention to the 20% of the customers who account for 80% of the business and worrying about the other 80% of the customers only as time or resources permit.

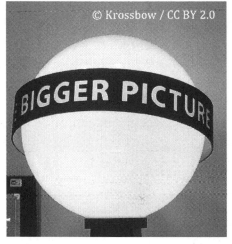

Though the 80/20 rule is not always universal, it makes the most sense to focus on the place where you will have the greatest effect with the minimal amount of effort. This will free you from the minutia that will require a great amount of effort to achieve only a small possible success. This is another very important aspect of seeing the big picture.

This Skill in Action

When David first arrived at his current job with the Mill Valley Public Library, he met Anne Montgomery, who was the city librarian for Mill Valley. Anne started her career as an entry-level technical services librarian, but moved steadily up the organizational ladder by taking on increasing responsibilities and a greater focus on management with every new position she acquired.

This is not unusual. Moving up the chain of command within the library world is a typical career path for many librarians, but it was what happened afterward that made Anne Montgomery's case so interesting. At the request of Anne's supervisor, Anne began managing other departments in the city, such as the Parks and Recreation Department, the Fire Department, etc., when those managers were on vacation. Then Anne was promoted to assistant city manager and finally to city manager. A librarian managing an entire town — imagine that!

When David asked Anne how she did it — how did she rise so steadily from technical services librarian to city librarian and then to city manager? — she told him that being able to see the big picture consistently was one of the major reasons why she had been promoted or landed jobs with increasing responsibility throughout her career, eventually rising to the top job in the organization.

Tips to Acquire This Skill

As we've already pointed out, acquiring this skill is something that probably cannot be taught, but it can be acquired through practice, experience, being aware, and keeping the big picture always top of mind. To see the big picture, librarians and information professionals need to step out of their traditional roles and imagine themselves as president or chief executive officer of that company or organization.

The top executive in a corporation or other organization is always focused on the welfare of the entire entity, the long term, and not getting bogged down in the minutia of detail. If you also aspire to be recognized as an important contributor and to move up the organizational ladder, you need to start thinking as a high-level executive, taking responsibility for meeting the goals of the entire organization.

Further Reading

1. Cope, K. (2012). *Seeing the big picture: Business acumen to build your credibility, career, and company*. Austin, TX.: Greenleaf Book Group Press.
2. Stanier, M. (2010). *Do more great work: Stop the busywork, and start the work that matters*. New York, NY: Workman Publishing Company.

CHAPTER 6

Business and Management Skills

You Need to Expand Your Career Potential

Now, with Jill Hurst-Wahl's advice in mind regarding the non–library related skills that differentiate librarian and information professional employment candidates, we move into the all-important area of business skills.

You don't need to have an MBA, but you do need to think like a business person and speak their language, regardless of the type of library or organization where you work now or in the future.

Here are 16 of the most important business skills to master. You may already possess some of these skills, but this is a good time to take inventory and refill your toolbox.

Skill #23: Marketing and Sales

Description

When we present the marketing and sales skill at our workshops, we often encounter indifference or even resistance from some librarians and information professionals who clearly feel they have no need to learn, nor any interest in learning, these most basic and fundamental business skills. While librarians and information professionals may never find themselves selling soap, toothpaste, or some other commodity, it is extremely important to remember that you are always selling a product and it is the most valuable product you have to sell. Every minute of every working day, librarians and information professionals are selling themselves, their credibility, and the importance of the service they provide — finding information and, more importantly, solutions to a customer's problem.

Contrary to what some librarians and information professionals would like to believe, marketing and selling skills are some of the most important skills you can learn and may often be the make or break decision in landing a new job or keeping the one you have when budget cuts occur.

In many ways, librarians and information professionals are a lot like consultants or other types of professionals who provide guidance and advice. Consultants are paid big bucks to perform a service that a client cannot do and to provide solutions to that customer's problems. But many librarians and information professionals don't realize the great value they provide to a customer who lacks the skills we have to find on-target, relevant, and current information that provides the solution to their problem.

We need to recognize the value we provide and we need to constantly educate our customers and make them aware of the value they are getting from us. All too often, librarians and informational professionals make the grave error of assuming that their customers already know the high value of the service we provide.

When you are lucky enough to have a client who intuitively recognizes the value they are receiving from you, that is fantastic. But more often than not, customers, supervisors, peers, and many of the people you encounter will need to be taught and reminded, again and again, why you, your department, and the services you provide are so vital and critical to the  organization. Marketing and selling are the skills you need to master and practice to make clients, stakeholders, and others understand the value you provide.

It should be dually noted that the marketing and sales skill you need to communicate your value to your customers is the same skill you need within your organization when you are vying for new resources, seeking to obtain funds to purchase furniture or equipment, jockeying for high priority and funding for one of your projects, or in so many other situations where conveying your value is of utmost importance.

Tips to Acquire This Skill

Thousands of books are written on marketing and sales and if you look around you will see numerous courses and training sessions on selling and marketing techniques, both in the library world and beyond. Many organizations also provide marketing and sales training to all employees with the notion that everyone in that organization is a salesperson for whatever product or service they sell.

You can learn many great marketing and sales techniques by taking a class or reading a book. Another great way to learn good marketing and sales fundamentals is by asking someone who is a marketing or sales professional. Perhaps one of the marketing or sales professionals in your organization would be amenable to discussing some of their techniques with you or mentoring you.

Beyond readings, classes, and obtaining professional advice, the very first step librarians and information professionals should take is to develop the mindset that everyone is your customer. Whether that person or organization you are serving is paying directly for the information and solutions you provide or whether that entity is benefitting from your services through indirect funding that underwrites your department and your job, the very first thing you can do to acquire marketing and sales skills is to think of everyone as a customer or a potential customer.

Even in the public library arena where David currently works, he considers everyone a customer and uses that word to address the visitors to his library. Once you start thinking of everyone as a customer, you will naturally begin to treat everyone as such, and you will be well on your way to unleashing the marketing and sales skills you already possess.

Further Reading

1. Dempsey, K. (2009). *The accidental library marketer.* Medford, NJ: Information Today, Inc.
2. Dowd, N., Evangeliste, M. & Silberman, J. (2010). *Bite-sized marketing: Realistic solutions for the overworked librarian.* Chicago, IL: American Library Association.
3. James, R. D. (2011). *Public relations and marketing for archives: A how-to-do-it manual.* Chicago, IL: Society of American Archivists.
4. Potter, N. (2012). *The library marketing toolkit.* London, UK: Facet Publishing.
5. Smallwood, C. (2012). *Marketing your library: Tips and tools that work.* Jefferson, NC: McFarland & Company, Inc., Publishers.

Skill #24: People Management

> *"Managers handle tasks and timetables and make sure things get done. Leaders have a vision, and they engage and challenge employees to enroll in it. They set a tone for the company and they define the culture and the values, and make sure the managers are managing to the vision, culture, values."* —David Kaiser, Dark Matter Consulting

Description

Another important business skill that makes many librarians and information professionals uncomfortable is the job of supervising others. While we recognize that some librarians and information professionals may have no interest in being a supervisor, we'd like to make the case why people management skills are extremely important, even for those who will never manage anyone, and why managing people can be a necessity for anyone interested in moving up the organizational ladder In their career.

You may wonder why we believe people management skills are very important even for those who have no interest or intentions in managing others and no ambition to move up the organizational ladder. It's because management is all about two things: (1) motivating other people and (2) delegating responsibility. Even if you never formally have people under you in the organization chart or if you are a solo librarian and don't expect that situation to change, it is highly likely that at least some time in your career, you will be working with other people in a way where motivating and delegating become very important skills.

In most MBA programs, students are often assigned to small groups to work on projects or solve theoretical problems. While many people dislike the idea of being paired with a few other individuals they may not know or may not even like, this exercise is performed over and over again because in the real world participating in groups is a fact of life. This is true whether you are working in a corporate setting, a nonprofit organization, a government job, an academic environment, or even in the public library sector. People from different parts of the organization, with many diverse skills and few commonalities are often thrown together to work on a task force or a committee with some purpose that will benefit the entire organization.

In those situations, you will find yourself where you have no control or authority to dictate what others should do, but your chances of success or failure and your reputation within your organization will be tied to how well you are able to 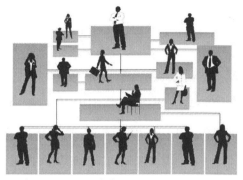 get others to collaborate to reach a successful outcome. Knowing how to motivate others and successfully delegate tasks is a management skill in action.

Even if you don't ever find yourself in a group situation like the one described above, you will likely find yourself in a situation where your success is directly tied to motivating and delegating a task to another coworker or a vendor and your ability to manage that person successfully is critical.

For those who do want to move up the organizational ladder, you will most certainly find yourself managing other individuals some day and the sooner you acquire some people management skills, the more your chances of success. As a people manager, you will quickly learn that being successful is about getting things done, and that requires leadership, motivation, and delegation.

Of the many responsibilities of a manager, delegation is often the most difficult for many managers to master because it involves relinquishing control, letting go, and depending on the success of a subordinate. But managers can't do everything themselves. They need to delegate and depend on others to help them accomplish their tasks and successfully complete their projects. The more they are able to delegate, the more they are able to accomplish.

Of course, delegation alone isn't a guarantee that people will perform satisfactorily. People have to like what they're doing, they have to have the capability to perform the job successfully, and they need to feel motivated to do the job. It is the job of the manager to motivate their staff.

Tips to Acquire This Skill

Like marketing and sales, thousands of books have been written about managing people, and classes and workshops on people management are everywhere.

While not downplaying the value of taking a course or reading a book on people management, we believe that the key to successful people management is the ability to motivate and delegate. Although many techniques abound for ways to motivate people, we believe that everyone is motivated by different forces, so a successful manager will take the time to figure out what motivates each of their staff members and then try to feed that individual's needs in order to keep that person motivated.

Delegating involves learning to trust subordinates and letting go, which is difficult for many managers to do. We believe if you are successful in pairing competent people with tasks they want to do and giving those individuals the support they need to successfully complete their tasks, you will be applying the two main principles of people management: motivating and delegating successfully. And that will make you a better people manager and leader.

Further Reading

1. Evans, G. E. & Alire, C. (2013). *Management basics for information professionals* (3rd ed.). Chicago, IL: ALA Neal-Schuman

2. O'Neil, S. & Kulisek, J. (2011) *Bare knuckle people management: Creating success with the team you have.* Dallas, TX: BenBella Books, Inc.
3. Rother, M. (2010) Toyota Kata: *Managing people for improvement, adaptiveness and superior results.* New York, NY: McGraw Hill Education.
4. Buckingham, M. & Coffman, C. (1999). *First, break all the rules: What the world's greatest managers do differently.* New York, NY: Simon & Schuster.
5. Buckingham, M. & Clifton, D. O. (2001). *Now, discover your strengths.* New York, NY: Simon & Schuster.

Skill #25: Volunteer Recruiting and Management

> *"There will be no greater advocate for your library than a trained and happy volunteer." (Mid-Hudson Library System, 2005).*

Description

Although volunteer recruiting and management sounds like it should have been included in the previous section on "People Management" (Skill #24), we have decided to present this as its own unique skill because it is one that deploys a completely different set of tactics and produces benefits that can give any librarian or information professional an additional competitive edge.

In Skill #24, we discussed how managing people can be an important skill for everyone, but especially so for those interested in moving up the organizational ladder. We also asserted that delegating and motivating others to do the work can help you accomplish so much more than what you can do as an individual.

Hiring and managing volunteers can produce the same effect, with no additional cost. If you have a limited budget or no funds at all for hiring paid employees, adding in a volunteer workforce can expand your project and other capabilities. Hiring a volunteer workforce is one way to weather an economic downturn or budget cuts at your organization. In fact, in a tough economy or a recession, the availability and quality of potential volunteers increases, as a higher number of skilled people are no longer part of the workforce.

Additionally, if you are seeking to break into the management arena, but have little or no supervisory experience, creating a volunteer workforce can give you a real people management experience to add to your resume.

This Skill in Action

In David's local History Room within the Mill Valley Public Library, there has never been a budget to hire any additional help. But David has created his own volunteer workforce that has at times swelled to as many as 35 people. Some volunteers may only work a few days per month, while others may work as much as 20 hours per week.

This has allowed David to take on an enormous digitization project of the archives for the City of Mill Valley. David's volunteers are busy digitizing vintage photographs, maps, oral histories, articles, and even books as well as creating a biographical and geographical database of information about all of the people, houses, and buildings in Mill Valley, past and present.

Additionally, David's volunteer staff are building indexes and creating unique new reference tools to help researchers find information on the town's heritage. All of this information is being made available through the library's website as well as through exhibits inside the library curated by History Room volunteer staff.

Tips to Acquire This Skill

Acquiring this skill is as easy as placing an advertisement in a local newspaper, posting to a library listserv, or putting a notice on your library's website that you are seeking volunteers. Volunteers can be professionals from within the library world or those  with a myriad of skills from outside the library profession. David's volunteer workforce includes both student and mid-career practitioners who may be librarians, archivists, or other types of information professionals as well as many docents from the neighborhood or neighboring towns.

What draws library science and archival students and unemployed or practicing librarians to want to volunteer in a setting like David's local History Room is the potential to learn new skills and gain real-world experience in such areas as digitization, digital archiving, electronic indexing, and other areas where they lack those skills. Many of David's interns have gone on to find great jobs after interning in the History Room, but along the way they helped David build databases and do things he could never accomplish if he was just a solo librarian.

Though David has had many decades of experience in people management, some of David's best interns and docents have helped him by training and supervising newer interns and docents, thus giving those volunteers real-world people management skills they can add to their resumes.

Further Reading

1. Evans, G. E. & Alire, C. (2013). *Management basics for information professionals* (3rd ed.). Chicago, IL: ALA Neal-Schuman

2. Driggers. P. F. & Dumas, E. (2002). *Managing library volunteers: a practical toolkit*. Chicago, IL: American Library Association.

Skill #26: Strategic Planning and Policy Development

> *"We have to constantly identify new ways that we can add value to our services and build the loyalty of our clients."*
> *(Bates, 2011)*

Definition

Strategic planning is an organization's process of defining its strategy or direction and making decisions on allocating its resources to pursue this strategy and resulting policies. In order to determine the direction of the organization, it is necessary to understand its current position and the possible avenues through which it can pursue a particular course of action. Generally, strategic planning deals with at least one of three key questions:

- What do we do?
- For whom do we do it?
- How do we excel?

In many organizations, this is viewed as a process for determining where an organization is going over the next year or, more typically, three to five years. Strategic planning can lead to new policies to meet and support the direction of the organization.

Description

If you don't know where you're going, you won't get there. You must have a mission, goals, and objectives that align with the organization and revisit them frequently to make sure they are still relevant, update them as needed, and evaluate how we are doing at meeting or exceeding them. You may be thinking that this is yet one more thing to add to your plate. But, if you don't do this for your segment of the organization, your own career, or the organization at large, you will be left behind as others move forward with the new direction and strategy of the organization.

Tips to Acquire This Skill

Many of the skills mentioned in this book, such as effective writing, active listening, problem solving, communications, and implementing successful change, are key to strategic planning and policy development. Start small. Even if your own organization is not actively planning strategically (though you can bet they are), do it in your own area of the organization. Making a difference will allow you to develop your planning and policy skills. Add in good communications about what you are doing and show ROI (return on investment) and you'll get the recognition that will make your position more secure and your input more valuable. If you are volunteering in an organization, offer to chair or be on a committee for strategic planning and policy development. You'll add valuable skills to your toolbox and your resume.

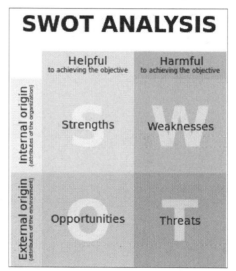

Further Reading

1. Bates, M. E. (2011). Think strategically: Add value to your business. *Bulletin*, 37(3), 43-45. Retrieved from batesinfo.com/Writing/Writing/articles_files/asist-adding-value.pdf

2. Nelson, S. (2008). *Strategic planning for results*. Chicago, IL: American Library Association

3. Platt, N. (2011). Staffing studies are a crucial part of strategic planning. Retrieved from http://strategiclibrarian.com/

4. Staley, D. J. (2012). Futuring, strategic planning and shared awareness: An Ohio University Libraries' case study. *The Journal of Academic Librarianship*, 38(1), 1-5.

Skill #27: Financial and Budget Management

Description

As librarians and information professionals move up the organizational ladder, the ability to construct and manage a budget becomes critical. You will need to accurately estimate your department's costs and any revenues you might bring in. As a department or project manager, you will be asked to:

- Prepare a defensible budget
- Develop a sound financial plan
- Show you are fiscally responsible
- Demonstrate why you need money for projects or major purchases
- Live within your means and achieve the numbers established in your financial plans

Consistently submitting responsible financial plans and bringing costs for your department in at budgeted levels can be the difference between success and failure. Additionally, you want to find ways keep your costs as low as possible, so that your department will not become an easy target during an economic downturn or other situation that precipitates a round of budget cuts.

Although it can often be difficult for libraries to find a way to become a profit center, the more you are able to turn your department into a revenue generator, the less likely your department will be a casualty when budget cuts occur.

If you can't find ways to directly generate revenue to offset the costs in your department, try to assess and quantify the value your department brings to the organization. For example, if your department provided valuable information that was critical to the launch of a new product, try to quantify the value you created by calculating the revenue that is being generated by that new product, which wouldn't have been built without your department's help.

If information solutions your department provided brought a new product to market much quicker than if they had to go outside the company to complete that research, try to compute the value of bringing that new product to market much quicker. If the organization would have had to pay a consultant or a highly paid internal staff member (who is not a researcher) to provide the information your department prepared if your department didn't exist, try to calculate that cost for outside help versus the expenses your department actually incurred. Use that differential to compute the financial value provided by your department. Departments that generate revenue or at least break even are less likely to suffer during a belt tightening exercise.

This Skill in Action

When David was brought on board to manage the local History Room in Mill Valley, he needed funding to purchase the software and equipment required to start and manage the digitization project. He also wanted the History Room to become self-sufficient, and eventually into a revenue generator for the library.

To achieve his goal, David established a business selling copies of vintage photographs from the History Room collection, local history books, and postcards with historic images of the library through time. David's goal is to gradually expand the number of local history book titles sold and add a new line of merchandise that would include posters and small souvenirs, such as a replica of the timetable for the railroad that ran through town more than a century ago.

David's eventual plan is to run a small retail gift shop in the local History Room as well as on the library's website. Does it seem strange that a public library might offer such an array of merchandise? Maybe so, but when times get tough and organizations look to cut costs, no one is going to eliminate or even downsize a department that is generating revenue.

Tips to Acquire This Skill

Like so many of the other business skills we are discussing in this chapter, lots of books have been written on the subject of budgeting and writing financial plans and many classes are offered to teach this skill. Additionally, librarians and information professionals might consult their colleagues to see how other librarians are managing their budgets and writing plans. Finally, it is always a good idea to establish a relationship with the finance department in your organization. That department can offer guidance and assistance in helping you prepare a sound budget and create the financial plans and other documents most commonly used for budgeting and financial planning within that organization.

As for the concept of generating revenue, you might start by looking at ways that other, similar libraries may be operating and how they might be making money. It's just a matter of looking at your situation and imagining what things you can do that may generate revenue or demonstrate value.

Further Reading

1. Stueart, R. D., Moran, B. B., & Morner, C. J. (2013). Library and information center management.
2. Warner, A. S. (1998). *Budgeting: A how-to-do-it manual for librarians*. New York, NY: Neal-Schuman.
3. Gordon, R. S. (2004). *The accidental library manager*. Medford, NJ: Information Today.

Skill #28: Communications

"You can have brilliant ideas but if you can't get them across, your ideas won't get you anywhere." —Lee Iacocca

Definition

Communication is how we exchange information between individuals or groups of people. Successful communication happens when both the sender and receiver understand the same information. Communication can be verbal or in writing.

Description

Most of the skills we discuss in this book have a communication component that is vital if we are to strengthen and demonstrate our value. Effective communication is a two-way process. We need to know what we want to say and why. Next we need to think about how we'll say it, but not just in words. Body language, eye contact, and tone of voice are important.

Communication goes both ways — we need to listen as well as speak. "Listen" is a key word here. We need to not only hear with our ears, but also listen attentively (see Skill #42, "Active Listening").

It's important to have a goal in mind for communication. What is the outcome you desire? Is it to reach an understanding, come to an agreement, or promote your value or that of your information center or library?

Depending with whom you are communicating, you will want to use language that is easily understood. If you are speaking to colleagues in the library world, using such phrases as MARC tags, LC subject headings, etc., is fine. If you are speaking to those outside the library realm, including stakeholders and budget gatekeepers, you want to communicate in terms they understand.

This Skill in Action

One of Deb's former students has decided to remain in her job in the insurance industry rather than seek a library or information industry job. Her company is expanding and she sees that there is a lot of opportunity to use her library and information professional skills in nontraditional ways. She has offered to create a departmental newsletter that her manager agrees is a great idea. It will contain tips on everything from how to find digital assets within the organization to using templates to get formatting correct on frequently used document types. She is showing initiative and creating a product that will communicate vital knowledge simply and in few words while demonstrating her skills.

Tips to Acquire This Skill

Take the time to practice good communication skills about subjects you are passionate about and want to share with others. This experience makes it easier when the subject may be more difficult to put into words or into a report or is one you don't feel comfortable talking about. If you communicate your value, ideas, and what everything you do brings to the table in your organization (remembering that others may not know the value you bring unless you tell and show them), it will become part of everything you do. Toot your own horn!

Further Reading

1. Mind Tools. How good are your communication skills? Speaking, listening, writing, and reading effectively. Retrieved from http://www.mindtools.com/pages/article/newCS_99.htm

2. Vendome, N. & McVey, J. J. D. (2012). *Effective communications in easy steps: Get the right message across at work.* Warkwickshire, UK: In Easy Steps Ltd.

3. What is good communication. Retrieved from http://www.people-communicating.com/what-is-good-communication.html

Skill #29: Public Speaking and Presenting

> *"According to most studies, people's number one fear is public speaking. Number two is death. Death is number two. Does that sound right? This means to the average person, if you go to a funeral, you're better off in the casket than doing the eulogy."* -- Jerry Seinfeld

Definition

Public speaking or presenting is the process of speaking to a group of people in a structured, deliberate manner intended to inform, influence, or entertain the listeners.

Description

Deb and David are passionate about what we do and about our profession. We use public speaking and presentations to share that passion with colleagues and clients to network, get work, and get recognition for our skills. You can, too.

In today's world, where much interaction is virtual, a face-to-face meeting or presentation is a valued commodity, but less common. We must be able to speak confidently both in person and virtually. Confidence in one's public speaking and presenting skills leads to strong interpersonal relationships, stimulating conversations, potential for career advancement, and reduced stress. Listeners regard good speakers as problem solvers and leaders.

Think for a moment about speakers and presentations that stick out in your mind. What was it about them or their presentation that made you remember them? Was it their passion and knowledge about their topic, were they a good storyteller, or did they speak about something important to you? As you identify what good speakers have in common, you can begin to think about how you can craft your presentations so that listeners care about what you are talking about.

This Skill in Action

Deb teaches part-time in a library technology paraprofessional degree program. The final project for one of her classes is to visit a library, archive, historical society, or other document repository and ask 13 questions of the staff there on such topics as where the budget comes from, who the governing body and audience is, etc. At the last class session, each student must turn in a three- to five-page written report and give a three- to five-minute oral presentation about the visit.

Many of Deb's students have never spoken in front of a group before and are terrified by this project; others feel they could not possibly speak for five minutes. Deb reassures them that they will be speaking in front of a friendly group, many of whom they already know or whom they will get to know as the class progresses. She encourages them to practice till they feel comfortable sharing. Deb also reminds them that this is great training for networking and job interviews.

On the final day of class, the students come ready to present. They have practiced in front of family members and even the family dog. They are so excited to share what they've learned that they cannot wait to speak. Many are not done at the five-minute mark and Deb has to stop their presentation so there will be time for all to speak.

What these students learn is that they can present if they are prepared and passionate about what they are talking about

Tips to Acquire This Skill

Most of us have to present reports to our boss or team. Even if oral reports are not required, think of ways you can add to a conversation. Do your homework and practice in front of a mirror, a trusted coworker, or family members. Start small. As you practice, you will gain confidence and it will become second nature to speak publicly. That said, be sure that you do your homework on your topic and can back up what you are saying.

If you volunteer in some way, you are already likely addressing others, making announcements, asking for donations, or contacting members. That is public speaking, but in a less formal way. We can grow our public speaking skills by starting small and going from there.

We may not always get to speak on a topic we love, but we can start with speaking at a local professional meeting, a book club and in many other ways. As we build our confidence, we will find it easier to do. It really does get easier with practice.

Many of us experience a sense of anxiety or even panic when asked to present to groups. Some good ways to become comfortable presenting include volunteering to read to children at the library or in an elementary classroom. Online forums, while not for making a speech, allow us to articulate our thoughts clearly, just as we would in a presentation. Attend free or low-cost events to see how other speakers use the podium as a stage to their advantage. Take notes and then incorporate one or two of those techniques into your presentations.

A great way to hone public speaking skills is by joining groups such as Toastmasters International. They have meetings all over the world at all times of day and the cost is minimal. See Further Reading below for information on finding a club near you.

Further Reading

1. Belicove , M. E. (2012). 5 tips on how to present like Steve Jobs. Retrieved from http://www.entrepreneur.com/blog/223513

2. Carnegie, D. (2009). *How to win friends and influence people*. New York, NY: Simon & Schuster.
3. Toastmasters International, http://www.toastmasters.org/, http://reports.toastmasters.org/findaclub/
4. Toastmasters International's 10 Tips for Public Speaking, http://www.toastmasters.org/tips.asp

Skill #30: Project Management

"The recent rapid proliferation of complex library services such as virtual reference and digital repositories suggests that the role of librarians is becoming increasingly project-oriented." (Kinkus, 2007)

Definition

A project, within an organization, is generally a temporary endeavor that has a defined beginning and end and a set of intermediate steps, all leading to a finite outcome with the achievement of definable goals. Project management is the management of that endeavor through the multiple stages of planning, organizing, securing, and managing resources to the successful completion of a specific task, subject to certain constraints, such as time, quality, scope, and budget.

Description

Project management is another essential business skill that cuts across all types of libraries and all kinds of organizations. As we've noted with a number of business skills presented earlier in this book, the need to perform successful project management becomes increasingly important as you move up the organizational ladder.

This is another business skill that isn't always embraced enthusiastically by librarians and information professionals. Nonetheless, librarians and information professionals need to know:

- How to define and manage a project from start to finish
- How to establish and achieve goals

- How to manage the project efficiently and effectively
- How to document what they did along the way

Tips to Acquire This Skill

Like most other business skills, much has been written on project management, and librarians and information professionals can also easily find a variety of classes and webinars on the subject.

Perhaps the best way to acquire project management skills is to actually participate in someone else's project and observe and learn whatever you can along the way. You can also join a project management team outside your organization, perhaps through a professional association or community or civic organization.

Further Reading

1. Kinkus, J. (2007). Project management skills: A literature review and content analysis of librarian position announcements. *College & Research Libraries*, 68(4), 352-363.
2. Allan, B. (2004). *Project management: Tools and techniques for today's LIS professional*. London: Facet.
3. Horine, G. (2013). *Project management: Absolute beginner's guide*. Indianapolis, IN: Que.
4. Portny, S. E. (2007). *Project management for dummies*. Hoboken, NJ: Wiley Pub.

Skill #31: Effective Writing

Description

Though it seems like such a simple and basic concept, quality, effective writing is an extremely important skill in any work environment. While the primary function of most librarians and information professionals may be providing research and reference services and administering some type of information collection, practitioners in any situation will likely need to communicate with management, other internal staff, customers, vendors, and other constituents on a regular basis. The ability to simply, succinctly, and accurately convey your message to the other party can be the critical deciding factor in receiving a new job offer, being considered for a promotion, or success and failure in general.

Some common documents you may need to write include:

- Periodic status reports for management on accomplishments and projects
- Proposals or requests for funding or justification of new or ongoing projects
- Internal requests for purchases or resources
- Budget proposals and reports
- Marketing materials and sales collateral to promote your products or services
- Information on the organization's website or social networking sites
- Job ads for recruiting paid or volunteer staff
- Performance reviews if you manage employees
- Email and text messages to management, other employees, vendors, or customers

Your writing doesn't have to be Pulitzer Prize quality, but it must meet the criteria test described above of simple, succinct, and accurate. Falling short in any of these areas may risk losing your audience and credibility inside or outside your organization. Typos, misspellings, poor grammar, and other mistakes are easily noticed, particularly with senior management, customers, and other important stakeholders. When readers are distracted by poor writing, they tend to miss the important points the author is trying to convey.

Additionally, when readers notice these types of errors in your writing, your competency comes into question. When someone reads a document filled with poor writing or mistakes, they may wonder if that is a sign that the author is careless in other situations, lacks  the ability to pay attention to detail, and does not take the time to be certain they are producing quality results on other projects and situations. A poor writer may lose funds, projects, promotions, customers, and even their job if that person is competing against another individual who writes well.

If a piece is well written, the reader may not notice the writing at all, but will and should be focused solely on the message in the document. On the other hand, if a piece is not well written, it will unfortunately be the poor writing that will stand out and be remembered in future situations.

This Skill in Action

David says that time and again, at every job he's had, he has seen those who write well get ahead in their careers. In the job-hunting arena, David says he's known many recruiters and human resources managers who immediately and unconditionally eliminate even those job candidates with excellent credentials if there are typos or poor grammar in their resumes or cover letters. Additionally, David has observed recruiters eliminate job applicants who are extremely verbose in their writings even if that person had the most relevant education and experience. Meanwhile, David has seen managers give the best assignments to those who write well, even if that person is not the most educated or experienced person.

Tips for Acquiring This Skill

Can someone learn how to write? This is a well-debated question among writers and academicians. While that debate may never be fully settled, as a former journalist, David believes that taking a number of steps can improve anyone's ability to write. The first step is to utilize the tools available in most word processing software packages that correct spelling and many grammatical errors and can also suggest synonyms or words to use to describe just about anything. Even if a program you might be using, such as email software, doesn't contain the tools to correct spelling and other errors, you can always compose your messages in a word-processing program that does have those features and export that text to your email once the corrections have been made.

Another simple step to improve your writing is to simply check your work carefully after writing something. During his days as a reporter, David always tried to come back later and review his stories again, if time permitted. David most often found mistakes or thought of better words or phrases to use when he had the time to review his work later or even the next day. When possible, Deb waits 24 hours after writing reports and more formal writings to let them "stew" a bit before reviewing and then submitting or sending them.

Another way to improve your writing is to enlist a second or third person to review, critique, and edit your work. Even as a professional writer, David always asked and still asks members of his staff to review documents he has written. But it doesn't have to be subordinates or coworkers. Friends and family can also be very helpful in reviewing and critiquing work.

Although librarians and information professionals can certainly take writing classes to try to improve their writing, a more effective way might be to find articles or books that specifically teach how to write a particular type of document. As a journalist and columnist, David's editors taught him much about the formula for writing newspaper articles and columns.

If you're called upon to write a five-year business plan for your library, a proposal to fund a project , a research paper, or just about any other type of document commonly used in the business world, remember that you are not the first person to write a plan or a specific type of paper. Libraries are filled with books, the internet is filled with websites, and many journals are filled with articles that give countless examples of those types of documents and explicit instructions and templates on how to write them.

Another way to improve your writing is to acquire an instructional or "style" book, which recommends editorial style and illustrates the conventions and standards in writing used by most professional publications. The *Associated Press Stylebook* and the *Chicago Manual of Style* are two of the most popular style books used by professional writers and journalists to improve their writing (see Further Reading below).

If you utilize the tools available in most word-processing software to correct spelling and grammatical errors, take the time to review your work, and develop a network of friends or colleagues who can serve as a second pair of eyes, you will find that your writing will improve and so will the opportunities in your career.

Further Reading

1. *Associated Press Stylebook*, https://www.apstylebook.com/
2. *Chicago Manual of Style*,
   http://www.chicagomanualofstyle.org/home.html

Skill #32: Writing Proposals for Fundraising and Grants

Definition

A proposal for funding or a grant is a simple request for funds that entails a description of a specific need and the proposed program that will fill that need.

Description

Learning how to write clear, concise proposals for funding can be a good career or part of a current job. Why? If you can bring money into your organization, you are perceived as invaluable.

Tips to Acquire This Skill

Volunteer in a professional association, the PTA, your workplace, or another organization to be part of a team that is writing a proposal for funding, be it a budget item or a grant. You'll utilize your information professional research skills to determine funding sources and how your needs match what they will fund. If possible, start by being on a committee and then move up to leading it.

An alternate or complementary way to acquire this skill is to be a grant reviewer. You'll learn what makes or breaks a grant or funding proposal and it will inform your own ability to write successful proposals.

Further Reading

1. Coley, S. M. (2013). *Proposal writing: Effective grantsmanship.* Thousand Oaks, CA: SAGE Publications.
2. Fritz, J. Better grant writing: From muddled to polished. Retrieved from http://nonprofit.about.com/od/foundationfundinggrants/tp/Grant-Writing-Tips-From-Muddled-To-Polished.htm
3. Rodriguez, C. Grant writing tips. Retrieved from http://www.dailywritingtips.com/grant-writing-tips/

Skill #33: Meeting and Event Planning

Definition

Meeting and event planners coordinate events such as meetings, trade shows, galas, and receptions. They find locations, arrange catering, entertainment, and transportation, and take care of all the details for the organization.

Description

Meeting and event planning can be fun, but also stressful. Planning and time management skills are important, as is making sure everyone who has a part follows through. Planning is largely people managing. Communication is key to make sure everyone on the team is on the same page. Attention to detail and flexibility will mean fewer last-minute surprises, but having a "Plan B" in your back pocket will save the day if something falls through at the last minute.

This Skill in Action

Several years ago, Deb was the conference coordinator for the annual AIIP.org conference. This was a volunteer position, but required a lot of work. Planning for everything from budgeting to food to a gala event was a wonderful, but exhausting adventure. Years later, Deb worked with her local SLA chapter on the hospitality committee and then led that group. Both experiences strengthened Deb's time management, organizational, project management, and people skills. Deb recommends starting small and not doing it backward as she did.

Tips to Acquire This Skill

Volunteer in a professional association, the PTA, your workplace, or other organization to plan programs or events. Look for programs or hospitality committees. Start small by being on a committee and then move up to leading it.

Further Reading

1. Allen, J. (2009). *Event planning: The ultimate guide to successful meetings, corporate events, fundraising galas, conferences, conventions, incentives and other special events*. Mississauga, ON: John Wiley & Sons Canada Ltd.
2. Event Checklist, http://www.wildapricot.com/membership-articles/eg-event-checklist

Skill #34: Contract Negotiations

Description

One of the universal conventions of doing business is the need to write, understand, and negotiate contracts. Even if you're a solo librarian or lone information professional working in the least complex environment, you will still need to negotiate contracts with all types of library vendors. Time and again, we

see appeals for help in negotiating contracts with vendors posted on the various listservs in the library world.

There are really two components to mastering contracts: One is understanding contracts and contractual language, and the second is the art of negotiating to get what you want. These are actually very diverse skills, but each one is an integral part of the process of creating and procuring good contracts.

Contractual language generally encompasses two parts. One part is the contractual language that is specific and unique to that agreement, spelling out terms and conditions for the product or service in question. The second part is what lawyers call "boilerplate," which is a standard, universal legalese language that goes into most contracts spelling out certain terms and conditions commonly found in contracts.

Tips to Acquire This Skill

Like most of the business skills in this book, the literature dealing with the art of negotiating is quite extensive and you can learn numerous techniques from books or articles on the subject, as well as classes and seminars offered by many organizations.

The main point to remember about contract negotiations is that it is a compromise for both parties. You have to know what's important to the other party and where they're willing to give as well as knowing your own deal-breakers and terms and conditions you are willing to negotiate in order to get what you want.

Similarly, there are numerous books and other publications explaining all of the standard contents of most contracts and the legalese boilerplates they contain. It would be useful to learn to understand the legalese, but when you create your own contract for something, you might simply lift this language from another existing contract.

Wherever you can, obtain copies of contracts from other libraries that use the same vendors or similar products, but be forewarned that some vendor contracts contain a nondisclosure clause that forbids the purchaser of those goods or services from disclosing the terms they have negotiated with that vendor.

Further Reading

1. Bond, R. F. (2013). *How to negotiate a killer job offer: The job "secret agent" series* (Vol. 1). Wayne, PA: World of Work Media.
2. Fisher, R., & Ury, W. (2012). *Getting to yes: Negotiating an agreement without giving in* (Rev ed.). London: Random House Business.
3. Tarrant, J. J., & Fargis, P. (1997). *Perks and parachutes: Negotiating your best possible employment deal, from salary and bonus to benefits and protection* (Rev. ed.). New York, NY: Times Business.

Skill #35: Decision Making

> *"Whenever you see a successful business, someone once made a courageous decision."* —Peter Drucker

Description

Many people might wonder how we could consider decision making to be a skill. Isn't it simple enough to make a decision? Well, it does sound simple, but if you spend enough time in the business world you will discover that many people have trouble making decisions, whether they realize it or not.

Many people, including a surprising number of high-level executives, are terrified to make a decision. Or perhaps they are terrified of making a wrong decision, and so they deploy a number of tactics to stall the decision-making process or find ways to take extra precautions to save their own skins if the decision they make ultimately leads to an adverse outcome.

An incredible amount of time and money is wasted in many organizations by managers who are afraid to make decisions. Some of these managers will research a topic to death, always finding new aspects that suddenly need to be investigated before moving forward. Other managers will enlist an enormous army of subordinates or coworkers from across the organization to solicit their input, and then conduct meeting after meeting, wasting the valuable time of many people in the organization, because that manager is insecure and afraid to make a decision. Still, other managers will even call in a very expensive consultant or consulting group and get them involved in the decision process, spending really big bucks in retaining that consultant and wasting more time before a decision is made, thus shirking their own responsibilities and covering themselves with the ability to blame the consultant if things go awry.

All of this inability to make a decision costs organizations astronomical amounts of money, with no evidence that delaying a decision will result in a higher success rate or that stalling tactics will bring about a better result.

In the business world, some actions will always succeed and some are destined to fail. Not every new idea can be successful and, despite sound research and adequate evaluation, there is often no way to predict in advance which ideas will succeed and which will fail.

It is always important to research an idea before a decision is made. And it's always a good idea to solicit the opinions of others who may be able to provide a unique viewpoint on a topic. An effective manager knows when to stop researching and soliciting other opinions and when it is just time to stop mulling the idea over and make the decision. Managers must accept that there is always risk in the business world and that procrastinating and waffling over a decision has a cost as well.

This Skill in Action

In the section on "Seeing the Big Picture" (Skill #22), we introduced you to Anne Montgomery, the former city librarian where David works in Mill Valley. She is a great success story of a technical services librarian who rose through the ranks to become city manager. When asked what she attributed to her success, Anne cited three management skills that she says she honed throughout her career:

- Delegating
- Accountability
- Decision making

Anne clearly saw her ability to make decisions — hopefully

good decisions, but decisions nonetheless — as a skill she had to learn along the way, rather than something that was an innate part of her being. She admitted that this was an acquired skill.

Anne made some brilliant decisions during her tenure as city librarian, such as seeing through the successful passage of a library bond issue that continues to provide income to the library today. Anne also tapped the community for additional funds and donations though a Library Foundation group that is completely separate from the governing Library Board or the Friends of the Library, who bring in $5,000 each month from their monthly book sale. These successes make Anne seem like a financial genius. But there must have also been some failures along the way. Anne wasn't afraid to make decisions and take some risk, whether that was procuring ongoing revenue streams for her library or taking on the role of interim manager of another city department that was completely separate from the library. Anne was consistently unafraid to make a decision and take on some risk, which reaped some really great rewards along the way.

Tips to Acquire This Skill

It seems like decision making should be an easy skill to acquire because making decisions seems black and white. But in reality, the skill of decision making resembles a softer, intangible skill that may be more difficult to teach than many other skills.

We believe that experience and observation are probably the best teachers of the decision-making skill. Just being aware of the potential costs of indecision and pulling other people into the decision-making process, and the recognition that there is such a thing as overanalyzing and over researching an issue, goes a long way toward avoiding decision paralysis.

Beyond that, just hearing success stories like Anne Montgomery's and understanding that managers need to sometimes take risks will make a better decision maker out of most of us.

Further Reading

1. *Harvard business review on making smart decisions.* (2011).
   Boston, MA.: Harvard Business Review Press.
2. Kahneman, D. (2011). *Thinking, fast and slow.* New York,
   NY: Farrar, Straus and Giroux.
3. Mash, S. D. (2010). *Decision-making in the absence of
   certainty: a study in the context of technology and the
   construction of 21st century academic libraries.* Chicago, IL:
   Association of College and Research Libraries.

Skill #36: Storytelling

"Storytelling can work as a pitch — for more money, for creating a new vision, and for setting a new direction. It is also a helpful and honest way to convey information from executives or the organization at large back to your staff. Essentially, it can become two-way communication through engagement and story sharing up and down the organizational hierarchy." (Schachter, 2008)

Definition

Storytelling is making something (a presentation, report, article, or conversation) engaging and memorable.

Description

Everyone has a story to tell. Good storytellers engage the listener and provide excitement and anticipation of the story outcome. Every information professional or librarian needs a cache of stories to support the work they and their libraries or information centers do. You don't need to create all the stories — gather testimonials touting the work you do and the value you bring to the organization. Don't be shy — ask for them in your organization, from clients, and on LinkedIn. Offer to do the same for others.

Tips to Acquire This Skill

What are you passionate about? It doesn't need to be work related. How many times have you shared with others stories about this passion? Likely they have remembered your story and it's a talking point when you see that person again. Now put yourself in the opposite situation and think about a friend, family member, or colleague who shared a story with you that you cannot forget because the storyteller was passionate about telling his or her story. Think about something you are passionate about in your work or in a work-related way, and craft a story that you can share. Practice makes perfect so don't give up. It will become easier as you do more storytelling.

Further Reading

1. Gordon, W. (2012).The science of storytelling: Why telling a story is the most powerful way to activate our brains. *Lifehacker*. Retrieved from http://ow.ly/l16ET
2. Mind Tools. Business story-telling: Using stories to inspire. Retrieved from http://www.mindtools.com/pages/article/BusinessStoryTelling.htm
3. Schachter, D. (2008). Information pro as storyteller for staff, patrons, management. *Information Outlook*, 12(2), 28-29.
4. Simmons, A. (2006). *The story factor* (2nd ed.). New York, NY: Basic Books.

Skill #37: Instruction and Teaching

Definition

Instruction and teaching can be formal or informal and aimed at imparting information or instructions to improve the recipient's performance or to help him or her attain a required level of knowledge or skill.

Description

There is an old proverb: "In teaching others we teach ourselves."

When we teach others, we become educated in a field or area of expertise. We may think we don't have a skill in a particular area, but once we research the topic, and experiment with and create a way to teach others, we will have learned enough to become more knowledgeable than those we teach. In other words, we learn by teaching.

This Skill in Action

A few years ago, David and Deb were talking about how many paths their careers have taken and how they were often asked by colleagues how they got to where they are now. David suggested we create a series of webinars and workshops to share with colleagues about skill sets needed, what had worked for us and for others, and the value we as librarians and information professionals bring to the table. That was the impetus for creating our "Expanding Your Career Potential" webinars and for writing this book. We are passionate about what we do and we know the information world is changing all around us. We took our passion and knowledge, worked to expand upon it, and continue to learn as we teach.

Tips to Acquire This Skill

Think about the skills you have or things you are passionate about and how you could share those skills or passions with others. Is there a skill you'd like to acquire or strengthen? All of these options provide a springboard for what you might teach others. Most of us as librarians and information professionals teach all the time when we answer reference or research queries, explain a research or reference tool to a user, colleague, or client, or even when we share with a friend something new we've just learned about.

Is there a skill or tool at work or in a volunteer setting that you see lacking that would contribute to the success of the organization while allowing you to shine? Don't be shy — take the plunge, learn what you can, and create a very simple lesson, cheat sheet, or pathfinder for others to follow. Offer to teach whenever the chance arises and be proactive when you see a need.

Further Reading

1. Allen, J. M. (200). Ten traits of terrific trainers. Retrieved from http://www.coachjim.com/articles/traitsofterrifictrainers.html

2. Bowman, S. L. (2008). *Training from the back of the room!: 65 ways to step aside and let them learn*. San Francisco, CA: John Wiley & Sons.

3. Stolovitch, H. D. (2011). *Telling ain't training*. American Society for Training & Development.

Skill #38: Don't Give Away the Store

Definition

Your expertise is worth a lot! Don't give it away. Ask for something in return — more funding, more salary, or more recognition.

Description

Have you ever worked with a customer or client and later learned that the person received recognition, a bonus, or even a promotion based on intelligence that you provided? Have you ever felt like you should have received a piece of that pie?

Too often we are so willing to provide information or solutions that we give away the store without expecting anything in return. Many of our colleagues tell us, "This is part of my job." That is true, but what do you get in return for providing intelligence and resources that make it possible for others to do their job and to shine? Are your ideas and expertise being hijacked by others with  no reference to your knowledge or part in the process and outcome? Do you get credit where credit is due?

This may be one of the most difficult things for us to do, but we must move away from assuming others will give us credit, and instead move toward recognition of the skills we have and bring to our organizations or clients. This will ensure our value to the organization and lead to more job security and the potential for more career options.

This Skill in Action

Deb has learned that conversations with potential clients as well as detailed proposals can give away too much information. One client, who seemed like a sure bet for a project, asked for a detailed proposal, which Deb provided. After reviewing the proposal, the client then told Deb they decided to do it in-house. Soon after, Deb learned that the client was going to use her proposed plan to implement the project. Deb was paid nothing for her time and effort.

Tips to Acquire This Skill

Ask for recommendations on LinkedIn and testimonials from your customers and clients that you can include in reports to your superiors, on your website, or as part of your brand. Start with folks you feel comfortable asking. You will likely be surprised that many you work with will be happy to do this.

Further Reading

1. Daffron, S. C. Care about customers, but don't give away the store. Retrieved from http://www.computorcompanion.com/LPMArticle.asp?ID=365
2. Podesta, D. How to demonstrate value to my company. Retrieved from http://conniepodesta.com/how-to-demonstrate-value-to-my-company/
3. Weliver D. E. (2008). 10 ways to demonstrate value to your employer. Retrieved from http://www.moneyunder30.com/21-ways-to-demonstrate-value-to-your-employer

CHAPTER 7

Interpersonal Skills

You Need to Expand Your Career Potential

Interpersonal skills are often considered soft skills that are not easy to teach or learn. However, one can indeed hone these essential skills that will lead to more job satisfaction and security and the potential for advancement in one's current organization or to a position in another one. Ask any employer or manager which skills they find lacking in job applicants and interpersonal skills are right at the top.

These seven skills are intertwined and fit together like a puzzle. Master them all and you will be top of mind for job advancement or a new position. Start with one or two and build from there.

Skill #39: Team Player

"The leaders who work most effectively, it seems to me, never say 'I.' And that's not because they have trained themselves not to say 'I.' They don't think 'I.' They think 'we'; they think 'team.' They understand their job to be to make the team function." —Peter Drucker

Description

In the previous chapter about business skills, we talked about the importance of working in groups in the "People Management" section (Skill #24). Related to working in groups is the concept of being a team player. Being a team player means always putting aside any rivalries or differences you might have with coworkers at your organization, as well as any personal aspirations you might have for recognition and individual career  advancement, and focusing instead on finding ways to achieve your organizational goals as a group without any one individual trying to take credit for group decisions and accomplishments.

Many people have difficulty acquiring and practicing this skill and frustration levels run high when you find yourself working with others who are not team players. However, we believe that in the long run, team players will be rewarded and everyone benefits from the success they create.

Tips to Acquire This Skill

Being a team player is really a mindset. You can read all of the business school textbooks and other books about working in the business world, but in the end, what works best is to continually ask yourself the question: "What do we need to do to create the most value for our organization?" If you start each day by asking that question, you will be moving in a direction that will make you a good team player and someone who has a reputation of always looking out for the good of the entire organization.

Further Reading

1. Cox , B. (2005). *52 secrets to being the best employee ever! An insider's guide to unlimited career success.* Santa Barbara, CA: Power Training Institute.
2. Heilig, J. M. (2013). Playing nice in the sandbox of life: Working on a team. Retrieved from http://ow.ly/lIGMB

Skill #40: Implementing Successful Change

> *"Information professionals need to appreciate change, if sometimes an unwelcome teacher, because it is always a learning experience." (Montgomery)*

Description

"Change" is one of the most difficult phenomena to deal with. It is human nature to resist change. But change is inevitable in the business world. Competitors are always developing new products and creating new challenges; new technologies change the realm of possibilities; consumer tastes and preferences change over time; and world events keep changing and reshaping the political as well as the economic conditions we must endure.

While adapting to change may be difficult for many, we'd like librarians and information professionals to see change not as a threat, but as an opportunity for career advancement.

One way change can present an opportunity for career growth is if you are the one implementing the change. If you are headed down the path to career growth and expansion by acquiring some of the skills presented in this book, you may well find yourself in a position on the other side of the equation as the person who is tasked with implementing change at your organization.

This Skill in Action

With the rapid growth of available online information, the newspaper industry is going through many changes and most of them have been very painful. Yet, note how Leigh Montgomery characterizes change in the quote at the beginning of this skill discussion.

Anne Montgomery, who we first introduced you to in Chapter

5 with "Seeing the Big Picture" (Skill #22) and again in Chapter 6 with "Decision Making" (Skill #35), says she implemented changes at each of her jobs along the way to becoming a city librarian and ultimately a city manager. The changes she implemented always got her department noticed and improved productivity, work flow, or other processes inside that organization.

David has also been a change agent everywhere he's worked. He's brought online searching to a chemical company; built bibliographic, graphic, and transactional online services and databases for a number of publishing companies and airlines; and is now bringing a local history room into the 21st century through the creation of a digital archive. At each step along the way, David embraced new technologies and developed skills and experience that were in great demand because few information professionals had possessed those skills at that time.

Trying to change existing processes and systems in well-established corporations was not an easy task and David certainly encountered his share of resistance, but in the end, change always wins. In the case of the publishing companies and airlines where David worked, they knew that they had to embrace the new technologies or they would fall behind their competitors who were embracing that change.

Tips to Acquire This Skill

Perhaps the best way to implement successful change is to accept that change is inevitable, prepare for it as best you can, embrace the change when it arrives, and ultimately be a leader in implementing change at your organization.

Leigh Montgomery offers another idea on how to implement successful change. She says that she constantly asks herself, "What do I need to learn as our business changes?"

At David's first job as a library technician, way back in the 1970s, online searching was a brand-new concept and the librarian there didn't want to learn how to use this new tool. But she was delighted when David expressed an interest in learning how to conduct online searches. It was at that point that David recognized that, no matter where he was, if he learned about the newest technologies at that time, he could advance his career while so many others sat idly by.

Further Reading

1. Curzon, S. C. (2005). *Managing change: A how-to-do-it manual for libraries.* Chicago, IL: Neal Schuman Publishers.
2. Lomenick, B. (2013). *The catalyst leader: 8 essentials for becoming a change maker.* Nashville, TN: Thomas Nelson.

Skill #41: Networking

> *"'Network, Network, Network' should be your personal mantra. Go to conferences, have business cards ready, get involved in your local library groups. Most importantly, take the time to consider which of your contacts you should meet. Being helpful to other networkers pays dividends!" (Baldwin, 2011)*

Description

While readers of this book may cherry pick those skills that interest them most, networking is one skill we strongly recommend that every librarian or information professional should master. Of all the possible strategies and tactics for job hunting, networking is by far the best way to find a new job.

Your objectives of networking should be to:

- Meet or communicate with as many people as you can
- Convey your skills and experience to each person you meet
- Tell each person you meet that you are looking for a job or for new ways to advance your career
- Ask the people you meet to introduce you to others who may have an open job or might be helpful to further your job search or your career advancement in general
- Exchange contact information, so you can always follow up with that person and they will know where to find you if they hear about a job opening at a later time

There are many ways to network and you should choose the networking methods that feel most comfortable to you. One excellent way to network is by joining and becoming active in one or more professional associations, such as the Special Libraries Association (SLA), the American Library Association (ALA), the Association of Independent Information Professionals (AIIP), or one of the literally hundreds of other library or information professional associations at the local or global level.

If association volunteer work is not your cup of tea, simply attending professional association meetings can be just as valuable for networking. Other popular methods of networking include email correspondence, one-on-one informational interviews, and communicating via social networking websites (see Skill #14).

We believe that attending professional association meetings or social events at both the local and global levels is one of the most efficient and effective ways to network. It is efficient because you can meet many new people in the course of a two-hour reception, dinner, or cocktail party, and it is effective because you are meeting people face to face, which will make them less likely to forget who you are and more confident in recommending you to someone else who might have an open job. Additionally, once you've had a conversation with someone at one of these events, they will often introduce you to others at that same event, which increases your credibility and makes networking even easier for you.

Unfortunately, many people are uncomfortable trolling through a crowded room of people they don't know. For those who are more reticent to approach another person in a room and strike up a conversation, the one-on-one informational interview may be a better alternative.

For an informational interview, you contact another colleague you may or may not know via email, telephone, or any other means and arrange to visit that person, most often within the other person's work environment, but it could also be over coffee or lunch. In this context, you can learn more about the other person's job or department, but you are also building credibility and conveying your desire to find a new job or advance your career. It's like a job interview without the pressure and it is also good practice for building your confidence and sharpening your interviewing skills.

Informational interviews work well when you are interviewing with someone who may be very prominent, well-known, well-established, or highly experienced in the field. But you can also simply find a colleague in the directory of a professional association who sounds interesting or works at an organization you admire. Contact that person because you are both members of the same association; that's a good enough reason for the two of you to meet.

Why is networking so effective? When someone posts a job, they might receive hundreds of resumes. In many cases they might receive far more applicants than they can evaluate and your resume may be stuck in the middle of that pile. But when someone has already met you or if another colleague they trust gives them  your name, it gets your resume out of the stack and into the much shorter list of potential job candidates who they are likely to interview.

There are two final thoughts about networking we'd like to share with you: First, always carry a stack of business cards with you, certainly when attending any professional events or informational interviews, but also even when you're not working, because you never know when you might meet someone who can help advance your career.

If you don't have business cards, you should have some printed up. For under $30, you can order a supply of customized business cards that should last you quite a while. Even if you don't currently have a job, your business card should give anyone enough information to contact you any time. You can also list the type of job you are seeking on your business card if you like.

Our second and final thought about networking: You've probably heard it said that the best time to look for a new job is when you don't need one. Well, we would recommend the same advice for networking. Even if you're happy with your current job and have no aspirations of doing anything else, we say that's the time you should begin networking, so your network will be in place at some later time when you do need it.

This Skill in Action

Nearly every job David has found in his career has come through networking. When David moved to Northern California he knew little about the area or where to begin his job search, so David began networking. First, he joined the two SLA chapters in the San Francisco Bay Area and identified the current presidents of each chapter through SLA's website. Then he contacted both chapter presidents and invited them to lunch.

One of those chapter presidents happened to be Deb, but they had never met before that lunch. Over lunch with Deb and the other chapter president, David learned about the recruiters in the area that specialized in library jobs and developed a list of resources he could contact to build his network of professional contacts in the Bay Area.

Next, David began going to SLA meetings in the San Francisco Bay Area. It was at one of those dinners, that David learned that the Mill Valley Public Library was searching for a History Room Librarian to construct an electronic archive for the city, the job that would soon become his own.

As you can surmise, this was not the first time David found a job by networking. After landing job after job in a 35+ year career, David quickly learned to have no hesitation in telling anyone and everyone he meets that he's looking for a new job and we recommend you do the same.

Countless books and articles have been written on how to network, and many of them will sharpen your technique, give you great lines to use to start a conversation, or teach you ways to boost your confidence. But to paraphrase Woody Allen, "Just showing up is 80% of life."

If that's true, then we would say that the other 20% is "just joining up." If you want to find your dream job or simply advance your career, we recommend joining every professional association you can and showing up at as many meetings and events as your schedule will permit.

Yes, for many people, entering a room full of strangers can be a terrifying experience initially, but that feeling is temporary. If you are shy or reticent standing alone at the cocktail party, we recommend approaching someone else who is standing alone. Chances are that person will be delighted that someone wants to talk with them and once you make one new friend, it may feel easier to meet others.

As another tactic, when you arrive at the event and check in at the registration desk to pick up your name tag, tell the person at the registration desk that you're new and don't know anyone. We guarantee you will be introduced to many attendees and begin building your network very fast.

Further Reading

1. Baldwin, M. (2011). Marketing & presentation. Future Ready 365. Retrieved from futureready365.sla.org/12/12/marketing-presentation/
2. Calcagno, E. (2013).Exercise your leadership skills: Lead the change. *Library Journal*. Retrieved from http://ow.ly/lIGSh
3. Gordon, R. S. (2008). Networking for the busy information professional: Fostering relationships despite everyday obstacles. Retrieved from http://lisjobs.com/career_trends/?p=489

Skill #42: Active Listening

> *"Without listening, there is no flow in the discussion or building of ideas: just random thoughts that don't connect to each other. Vital information and good ideas are lost; we don't explore issues thoroughly." (Hamlin, 2006)*

Definition

"We have two ears and only one tongue, in order that we may hear more and speak less" — Diogenes Laertius

Diogenes hit the nail on the head. Active listening means fully concentrating on what is being said using as many senses as possible and giving full attention to the speaker.

Description

Skill #28, "Communications," addresses how we as speakers communicate. Active listening is just as important. In our busy lives, so many things are tugging at our attention that it can be difficult to really focus on what someone is telling us. How many times have we attended a webinar, only to be checking email or a website during the presentation? It isn't easy to stay focused with so many distractions and limited time.

However, when we don't actively listen, we miss out on truly understanding and internalizing the message, whether online or in-person. Patience to actively listen, allowing the speaker to pause without jumping in to speak, and providing verbal and nonverbal cues, such as nodding your head or simply saying "mmm hmm" encourages the speaker and also allows you to process what is being said.

This Skill in Action

Leigh Montgomery, librarian at the *Christian Science Monitor*, uses active listening to look for:

- Common aspirations in digital and quality journalism
- Patterns in how her managers talk about and use information in order to learn what's important to them
- Phrases that are subtle but important, like her manager stressing the importance of "being as close to the pipeline as possible"
- What is okay to do and what is not okay to do
- Books and articles her managers admired or concepts they endorse; she will write them down to read and use later in her work

Tips to Acquire This Skill

In every conversation you have over the next three days, practice active listening skills using verbal and nonverbal cues in response to the speaker, focusing on what is being said and only listening, not doing other tasks or thinking about what you'll have for lunch. This can be challenging if the person speaking is someone you don't get along with, is not a good communicator, or is talking about a subject you don't care about. However, you may find out that there is a project you can contribute to, an opportunity for career advancement, or some other important topic you may have missed if you were only passively or distractedly listening.

Further Reading

1. Active listening: Hear what people are really saying. Retrieved from http://www.mindtools.com/CommSkll/ActiveListening.htm
2. Hamlin, S. (2006). *How to talk so people listen: connecting in today's workplace*. New York, NY: Collins.
3. Hardman, E. (2012). *Active listening 101: How to turn down your volume to turn up your communication skills*. Amazon Digital Services, Inc.
4. Skills you need: Active listening. Retrieved from http://www.skillsyouneed.com/ips/active-listening.html

Skill #43: Empathy/Seeing the World Through Others' Eyes

Definition

Empathy is the ability to sense other people's emotions, coupled with the ability to imagine what someone else might be thinking or feeling. It doesn't mean feeling sorry for someone.

Description

Empathy entails self-awareness, being nonjudgmental, active listening, and self-confidence. Tone of voice, body language, and facial expression all convey to those we interact with how we are rejecting or accepting them or what they are saying. It is valued in both professional and personal relationships as it leads to bonds of trust, insights into what others are saying and feeling, and informs our decisions and actions.

Think of a really good reference interview and all the things that go into it: active listening, gentle questioning to get at what is really being asked, and then feedback to make sure the question is understood so the best solution or answer can be found.

This Skill in Action

One afternoon, Deb was on the reference desk of a public university when a member of the public approached. He wanted to know all about bighorn sheep, where they lived, when they migrated, that sort of thing. Deb was really excited as she had never seen them and had learned they were in the mountains nearby. As she helped this patron, she learned that he was planning to lead a hunting expedition, which shocked her, but ethically she knew she had to provide the correct information the patron was seeking and try to be empathetic to his feelings.

Tips to Acquire This Skill

This is a soft skill that leads to tangible results. It requires practice, even when we don't feel quite empathetic to someone's research or other request, or perhaps don't even like the person. Utilize many other skills in this book, such as active listening, communications, and a positive attitude to get to empathy. Put yourself in the other person's shoes.

Further Reading

1. Goleman, D. (2000). *Working with emotional intelligence.* New York, NY: Bantam.
2. Inam, H. (2013). The role of empathy in business success. Retrieved from http://ow.ly/lIHfn
3. Tahmincioglu, E. (2009). Empathy can go a long way at the office. Retrieved from http://ow.ly/lIHlm

Skill #44: Interviewer/Interviewee

Definition

When we think of an interview, we mostly think of the formal process where an applicant is evaluated for suitability for a position of employment. An interview also entails the interviewee sizing up the employer and the job opportunity, so in a way, the employer is also being interviewed.

Description

Most of us have sat on the interviewee side of the table, but there are skills that are required on both sides.

As the interviewee, there are many ways to best prepare for an interview:

- Research the organization thoroughly
- For an in-person interview, visit the interview location a few days before the appointment so that you can get the lay of the land as far as driving or public transit time, parking, which entrance to use, how people going in and out of the organization are dressed, etc.
- Practice mock interviews, answering those dreaded questions such as "What are your weaknesses?"
- Ensure your interview attire is clean and pressed and your hair trimmed
- Create a list of 3-4 relevant questions to ask the interviewer(s)
- Prepare a closing statement that will make you memorable in a good way
- Get a good night's rest the night before
- Prepare a portfolio or folder with copies of your resume, a notepad, and two pens (in case one goes dry)

On the day of the interview:

- Leave plenty of time to get ready so you are not rushed and stressed (you will likely already feel some stress, so no use making it worse)
- Do a full-length mirror check
- Arrive 10 minutes early
- Breathe deeply, stay calm, and be yourself
- Be honest, listen carefully, and take a moment or two to reflect before answering questions
- As soon as possible after the interview is over, write down your impressions, things you forgot to ask or say, and anything else while it is fresh in your mind. This will help you on future interviews and also provide content for your thank you note.

THAT evening, write a handwritten thank you note indicating you are still interested in the position and send it off the following morning.

If you don't get the job, don't be discouraged. Take this opportunity to evaluate your job search plan and make any needed revisions.

It is important to note that we are actually informally interviewing others and being interviewed or evaluated everyday on the job and in our professional and personal relationships. Remember, always act professionally so that you stand in good stead with your current employer for internal promotions and with potential employers and clients.

Tips to Acquire This Skill

Be prepared! That is the best strategy. Network at events, practice informal interviewing skills as you give your elevator pitch, and listen to how others give theirs. Ask a friend, family member, or colleague to do mock interviews with some questions you have prepared or found online. If you can do this with someone in our field, all the better, as they will have a good grasp of what is required for the kinds of positions we seek. Have them include some questions you didn't prepare to answer. Practice your closing statement so you know it by heart.

Further Reading

1. Freeman, A. (2013). *How to get job interviews in 2013: Master the 8 secrets to getting selected in today's competitive job market.* Amazon Digital Services, Inc.
2. Job Interview Questions Database for Job-Seekers, http://www.quintcareers.com/interview_question_database/
3. Monster.com career advice: Interviewing. Retrieved from http://career-advice.monster.com/job-interview/careers.aspx
4. Thank you letters. Retrieved from http://jobsearch.about.com/od/thankyouletters/a/thankyouletters.htm

Skill #45: Getting Buy-In

Definition

Getting buy-in is the art of getting the people you need to influence to go along with your ideas, recommendations, advice, or projects. Those people you need to influence might be your manager, coworkers, subordinates, customers, suppliers, or anyone else.

Description

Sooner or later, librarians and information professionals will find themselves in situations where they must obtain the approval, consent, or support of others to complete a project or accomplish their goals. Learning how to methodically and consistently get others to go along with your ideas and support you can be critical to your success.

One way to consistently get buy-in is to boost your credibility. In today's fast-paced world, senior management and others are often inundated with information. Everyone is having a tough time  sorting the hype from the genuine trends and strategic knowledge. This presents an opportunity for librarians and information professionals that will not only help your management and your organization, but will also give you the ability to obtain buy-in consistently.

You need to take advantage of this situation by becoming an expert on the topics that interest your management most. You want to develop the expertise, but even more importantly, you want to build that perception, so your senior managers recognize your expertise on those topics. This boosts your credibility to management and will make it easier to get buy-in when you need it.

To be recognized as the expert, you need to always be ready to share valuable information when asked or even before being asked. To position yourself to be ready, stay highly visible and communicate regularly with top management in person, by phone, email, Twitter, or whatever means is preferred by your management. Please note that it isn't about your favorite method of communication; you must use the channels preferred by your management.

If you can become the "go to" person for both inside and outside information, and if management knows they can not only trust you, but you can also connect them with experts in the field when they need to get up to speed on a topic, they will always call upon you.

If you follow these simple guidelines and do these things regularly, you will build trust and credibility with management and it will be much easier to obtain support for your ideas and projects and procure buy-in when you need it.

This Skill in Action

Leigh Montgomery has her own tactics for obtaining buy-in from her management. Here is how she proactively builds her credibility so it will be easier to obtain buy-in from her management when she needs it:

- Leigh sets quarterly goals based on her manager's goals, so they are both working toward the same end
- Leigh looks for opportunities to include things that motivate her and situations where she can apply her abilities, while still supporting the company's objectives

- Leigh always maintains revenue streams as a goal and always quantifies results because that is what her managers prefer
- As might be expected at a newspaper, Leigh's manager considers journalism to be the most important task in the company, so Leigh regularly takes the time to write articles and create content even though that is outside the job description of a newspaper librarian
- Leigh regularly communicates what she's accomplished and quantifies her achievements
- Leigh always tries to provide her managers with examples of where and how a librarian has made a difference
- Leigh listens for book titles, authors, articles, words, and concepts mentioned by her managers and writes them down so she can read them and become conversant with what is important to her managers

Tips to Acquire This Skill

Increasing your odds of obtaining buy-in is all about learning what is important to your management and then becoming an expert in those areas. Leigh Montgomery has outlined the many ways she learns what's important to her management in the "This Skill in Action" section above. If you adopt some of Leigh's methods of aligning herself with the interests of management, it will greatly increase your credibility and maximize your ability to obtain buy-in when you need it.

Further Reading

1. Blount, J. (2010). *People buy you: The real secret to what matters most in business.* Hoboken, NJ: John Wiley & Sons, Inc.

2. Kotter, J. P., & Whitehead, L. A. (2010). *Buy-in: Saving your good idea from getting shot down*. Boston, MA: Harvard Business Review Press.
3. Fisher, R., & Ury, W. (2012). *Getting to yes: Negotiating an agreement without giving in* (Rev ed.). London: Random House Business.

CHAPTER 8

Attitude Skills
You Need to Expand Your Career Potential

Interpersonal skills are often considered soft skills that are not easy to teach or learn. However, one can indeed hone these essential skills that will lead to more job satisfaction and security and the potential for advancement in one's current organization or to a position in another one. Ask any employer or manager which skills they find lacking in job applicants and interpersonal skills are right at the top.

These seven skills are intertwined and fit together like a puzzle. Master them all and you will be top of mind for job advancement or a new position. Start with one or two and build from there.

Skill #46: Positive Attitude

Description

Some librarians and information professionals may wonder why we consider maintaining a positive attitude to be a skill, but we strongly believe it is an important characteristic that employers seek in a candidate for a job or a promotion. Even if it's not explicitly stated in a job description, the presence or absence of a positive attitude in a job candidate becomes blatantly obvious in a job interview situation or in internal organizational meetings where managers are constantly evaluating current or prospective employees.

If you don't believe that maintaining and displaying a positive attitude is important, ask yourself this question: If you are hiring an assistant to help you achieve your goals and you interviewed two candidates with roughly the same credentials, but one displayed a positive attitude while the other seemed overly negative and pessimistic, perhaps even a bit cynical, which job candidate would you hire?

We also consider maintaining a positive attitude to be an important skill for career advancement, because we believe that like any skill, maintaining a positive attitude does not come naturally to many people, and that it takes a continuous effort and practice to hone and maintain a positive attitude, even in the face of adversity. Like any other tangible or intangible skills in this book, the librarian or information professional must want to acquire and maintain this skill and must readily acknowledge the critical significance a positive attitude can bring to anyone's career growth plans.

Unfortunately, not all librarians and information professionals agree on the importance of maintaining a positive attitude or perhaps they don't see that they have a negative attitude that is obvious to everyone else. When we perform our "Expand Your Career Potential" workshops, there are always a few participants who seem to come to the workshop with a negative attitude about their prospects for employment or promotion.

The first thing we do in our very first workshop is to ask everyone what excuses they have for not making a concerted effort to find a job if they're unemployed, or to secure a better job if they're underemployed or stuck in a rut and unhappy about their current job prospects. We then tell our audience that there really are no good excuses for why they can't acquire the skills they need or make the concerted effort to find their dream job.

But in spite of putting everyone through the "no excuses" exercise, there are always a few who may ask for guidance, but then have an immediate reason or excuse why that approach won't work when we offer them our best advice. And this is the essence and embodiment of a negative attitude put on display for all to see.

This Skill in Action

When we think of someone who epitomizes the embodiment of a positive attitude, we always think of Leigh Montgomery, the newspaper librarian from the *Christian Science Monitor*. In an ailing industry where probably only half of the newspaper libraries remain, Leigh and her library continue to thrive. While there are likely many different factors contributing to her success, the one characteristic that is immediately apparent when you meet Leigh is her positive attitude.

Like any other newspaper, the *Monitor* has had its share of economic issues. Although Leigh has seen many changes, new editors, and a library that has moved several times, she has found a positive point to stress: She says that all those moves the library has made in recent years have given her "great experience in library design."

Despite the economic troubles newspapers have experienced, Leigh has found a way to keep a positive attitude through it all — and that could be a major part of the reason why she still has a job as a newspaper librarian.

Tips to Acquire This Skill

So how should librarians and information professionals learn to acquire, maintain, and display a positive attitude? Well, first you have to truly want to have that positive attitude and believe that it will reap rewards that aren't likely with a negative attitude.

Beyond that, librarians and information professionals need to continually seek the positive, no matter how negative a situation may seem. You need to find ways to stress positive points and ignore the negative, like the way Leigh has turned all those library moves that would have annoyed and frustrated many librarians into a positive statement, like gaining a lot of experience in library design that may come in handy later in her career.

You need to always try to see the positive side of every situation, let the excuses go, and be fully cognizant of the attitude you are projecting in every business or career situation. And if you keep focusing on the positive points, it will become increasingly easier to own and retain that positive attitude.

Further Reading

1. Gordon, J. (2007). *The energy bus: 10 rules to fuel your life, work, and team with positive energy.* Hoboken, NJ: John Wiley & Sons, Inc.
2. Cox, B. (2005). *52 secrets to being the best employee ever! An insider's guide to unlimited career success.* Santa Barbara, CA: Power Training Institute.

Skill #47: Being Proactive

> *"Being proactive requires an active, open, seeking attitude, as well as reliable, high-quality action."* *(Scott, 2009)*

Description

When we discussed "Results Driven Problem Solving" (Skill #17) earlier in this book, we talked about how librarians and information professionals can no longer sit passively at the their desk simply providing information and how they must go beyond traditional reference and library work and develop the skill of problem solving.

Well, here is another skill librarians must develop to get out from behind the reference desk and the traditional role of a librarian. Librarians and information professionals must become proactive in working with customers or end users. In today's world, librarians and information professionals need to seek out their customers and end users on their turf, whether that means:

- Visiting the offices of their users
- Scheduling meetings with clients to learn more about their needs
- Advertising their services via social media or any other communications channel preferred by their customers
- Scheduling events to promote library services, or whatever works to attract new business

If we don't get up from our desks to increase awareness of the valuable services we as librarians and information professionals can provide, we may find ourselves without customers and ultimately without a job, if management believes we are expendable.

Unfortunately, many librarians and information professionals feel uncomfortable with this or don't know quite how to become proactive — but learning how to be proactive is really about learning a new skill. Every librarian or information professional needs this skill to survive in this new and complex environment.

This Skill in Action

To find a librarian who embraces the proactive skill and who has incorporated proactive techniques into her daily routine, once again, we need go no further than Leigh Montgomery, our newspaper librarian who is thriving in the face of adversity.

Being proactive is one of Leigh's mantras. She has been proactive in many ways throughout her career with the *Christian Science Monitor*. She has joined teams and committees outside the library. When the internet was first installed on all of the reporters' desktops in the newsroom, Leigh took it upon herself to teach the reporters how to use it. Leigh is proactive with her management, seeking them out before they come looking for her.

Leigh believes that her proactive stance has been instrumental in her success at the *Monitor* and she strongly encourages her library colleagues to become proactive. She says, "Those who sit around waiting for people to approach aren't around for long."

Tips to Acquire This Skill

It's simple to tell librarians and information professionals that they must become proactive, but for some this is alien territory — many of our colleagues are terrified at the thought of becoming proactive or don't really know how to make that transition.

For those who are extremely uncomfortable or frightened by the thought of becoming more proactive, it might help to identify colleagues who are taking proactive steps and look to see how they're doing it. Then try one proactive step at a time until you feel comfortable with that approach. For example, one of the proactive programs Leigh recommends is joining a committee or group of coworkers outside the library to plan an event or work on a specific project. If librarians and information professionals take this single step at their organizations, they will be on their way to becoming proactive and assuring their longevity with their current employer.

Further Reading

1. Scott, P. (2009). Promoting your professional development: The value of being proactive. *Info Career Trends*. Retrieved from http://lisjobs.com/career_trends/?p=598
2. Brophy, P. (2007). The proactive librarian. Retrieved from http://www.nb.rs/view_file.php?file_id=1941

Skill #48: Going Outside Your Comfort Zone

"The brave may not live forever, but the cautious do not live at all!" (Richard Branson)

Description

Many librarians and information professionals may feel a bit intimidated or uncomfortable in blazing ahead to new territory in order to become more proactive, as discussed in the previous section (Skill #47), and to take the steps necessary to acquire many of the skills presented in this book. These types of feelings are normal, but we strongly believe that developing the very skill that allows you to go outside your comfort zone from time to time can make a very positive impact on your career prospects.

Whether it is going outside of your comfort zone to develop some new skills or to do something else that causes you hesitation, learning how to safely go outside your comfort zone sometimes and gaining some successes in this area will make it easier and easier to step out of your comfort zone the next time an important opportunity presents itself.

This Skill in Action

Here again, when we heard Leigh Montgomery's many stories about how she challenges herself time and again to leave her comfort zone, we were extremely impressed with what we learned.

When Leigh joined the *Monitor*, she was originally a reporter without any education or experience in the library field, but when her managers encouraged her to apply for the librarian position, which became vacant, Leigh applied for the job even though it meant going out of her comfort zone. We find this particularly interesting because we are usually trying to convince librarians to go outside their comfort zones to perform a job not traditionally held by a librarian, and here is Leigh going outside her comfort zone to do a job that feels comfortable to all of us.

Leigh tries to go outside her comfort zone on a regular basis, which has included teaching a college class in journalism, taking a job at an outdoor outfitter store while she was in college, and learning a new sport each year, such as fly fishing.

Tips to Acquire This Skill

Most people are not nearly as highly motivated as Leigh Montgomery in challenging themselves repeatedly to go outside their comfort zone, but the illustrations in her story may give you some ideas of the many ways an individual could do so.

We would recommend starting slowly and finding something that may not be too terrifying and then trying that one thing that will take you outside your comfort zone.

If meeting new people is uncomfortable for you, as it is for many people, you might choose to go outside your comfort zone by establishing a goal to meet one new person you don't know at the next professional association meeting you attend. Or perhaps you could select one of the skills in this book and challenge yourself to acquire that skill as practice in going outside your comfort zone. In that way, you will actually be acquiring two new skills at the same time: the skill you chose to learn to take you out of your comfort zone and the skill of being able to go outside your comfort zone.

Further Reading

1. Dysart, J. I. (2005). Why libraries fail & tips for staying alive. *Feliciter*, 51(3).
2. Brown, C. B. (2012). *Daring greatly: How the courage to be vulnerable transforms the way we live, love, parent, and lead*. New York, NY: Gotham Books.

CHAPTER 9

Intangible Skills
You Need to Expand Your Career Potential

These intangible skills often don't appear on a job requirements list or in a job description, but they are often some of the most important in our field. As the world turns more and more toward Google instead of us, how can we ensure our continued value proposition in the organization or with clients? We must show the value that we bring over and above what Google provides and base that value on our skill set and more importantly on relationships of trust we build with our customers. As we build those relationships, we can demonstrate the value we bring to the organization, which will ensure our place in the organization and the continued support of our stakeholders.

Skill #49: Getting the Public to Come to Us Instead of Google or Wikipedia

> *"It's our job to show our clients the connection between our information sources and their strategic decisions... Our job is to get them to see that we are the missing link between information and actionable intelligence." (Bates, 2009)*

Definition

Librarians and information professionals are often bypassed by users who think they just need to use Google or Wikipedia to find all the information they need to do their work or studies. This is also known as "disintermediation," where we, as the middleman, are passed by. Rather than reacting to this with dismay, we need to be proactive and demonstrate the value our research skills bring to the table.

Description

Google doesn't translate to vetted research or enterprise search. Our clients often need file and data types that are not on the web at all, or are in the deep web (such as proprietary databases). The linking structure that makes up the fabric of the web does not always work for the information our users and clients need. We need to tell them this, over and over again, and prove it with the services and products we provide, such as value-added "Research and Analysis" (Skill #19), "Competitive Intelligence" (Skill #20), and other skills we cover in this book.

When we add in the granularity of power searching in such resources as Proquest Dialog or LexisNexis, we can get right to the heart of the matter at hand without handing our user or client hundreds of hits or information that is not relevant or on target.

Let them do the simple searches and come to us for the

difficult ones. We increase our value by making sure our expertise is best used to serve our clients.

This Skill in Action

Deb had a pharmaceutical client who asked her to search PubMed only because it was free. Deb explained that she uses Proquest Dialog to search Medline and Embase instead because the power search interface gets the exact results needed and PubMed doesn't cover the pharmaceutical literature as well as Embase does. While Medline has a low cost and Embase a higher one, it was much faster for Deb than paying her for an extended amount of her search time using PubMed.

Tips to Acquire This Skill

Using skills from this book, such as "Providing Value-Add Solutions" (Skill #18), "Communications" (Skill #28), "Don't Give Away the Store" (Skill #38), and "Storytelling" (Skill #36), we can demonstrate our value to users. Rather than wait for them to come to us, we must be proactive, anticipate research needs, and present them with strategic knowledge to  make their lives easier and to make them look good to their management or professor. They'll learn to come to us instead of only relying on Google. This is an ongoing effort to stay top of mind for the best, most relevant information that our expertise provides. We demonstrate value at our hourly rate finding what's needed while a higher paid attorney or manager spins her wheels trying to use Google, driving up costs and lowering productivity.

Further Reading

1. Badke, W. (2013). Teaching information cultures. *Online Searcher*, 37(2), 68-70.
2. Georgas, H. (2013). Google vs. the library: Student preferences and perceptions when doing research using Google and a federated search tool. *Portal: Libraries and the Academy*, 13(2), 165-185.
3. Shumaker, D. (2011). Disintermediation and the (embedded) librarian. Retrieved from http://embeddedlibrarian.com/2011/09/21/disintermediation-and-the-embedded-librarian/
4. Whelan, D. (2009). Librarians have value, even if libraries have less. Retrieved from http://ofaolain.com/blog/2009/07/26/librarians-have-value-even-if-libraries-have-less/

Skill #50: Building Trust with Management and Customers

Definition

Trust is reliance on and confidence in the integrity, strength, and ability of a person. It is the opposite of mistrust.

Description

Every worthwhile relationship is built on trust. It's easy to trust people you know and like, but more difficult for those whom you don't know well or don't get along with. Trust is an emotional skill, an active and dynamic part of our lives that we build and sustain with our promises, commitments, emotions, and integrity. We hope that others will be trustworthy. When someone betrays our trust, it is very difficult to trust them again.

We live in an era of mistrust. How can we build trust with management and customers? We must:

- Discuss and solve problems (and head them off) through direct, honest communication
- Share credit where credit is due and be generous in this
- Be honest when in doubt about our ability to complete a project or do so by a deadline
- Do what we say we will do
- Admit to being wrong and right wrongs
- Always tell the truth
- Trust others and express that trust in them

Trust builds upon many other skills we have discussed in this book: "Communications" (Skill #28), "Active Listening" (Skill #42), "Empathy" (Skill #43), and "Positive Attitude" (Skill #46).

This Skill in Action

Nelson Mandela is an iconic figure and someone who was betrayed in ways most of us cannot imagine. Yet he overcame distrust and betrayal to go on to be a world leader and inspiration to most of the world. He wrote: "Resentment is like drinking poison and then hoping it will kill your enemies."

Tips to Acquire This Skill

Trust can be scary because it exposes us to possible betrayal. Assuming everyone is trustworthy takes much less work than trying to figure out what someone's motives might be. There is risk in this, but life is too short to spend being suspicious. There will be those who betray us or cause us to lose trust in them. It is a horrible feeling when someone isn't trustworthy, but trust we must if we are to thrive. Be trustworthy and in most cases, that trust will come back to you. Try the steps above. You may be pleasantly surprised at the return on your effort.

Further Reading

1. Baker, C. (2007). Building trust in the workplace. Retrieved from http://biznik.com/articles/building-trust-in-the-workplace

2. Covey, S. M. R. How the best leaders build trust. Retrieved from http://www.leadershipnow.com/CoveyOnTrust.html

3. Solomon, R. C. (2003). *Building trust: In business, politics, relationships, and life*. New York, NY: Oxford University Press.

Skill #51: Quantifying, Demonstrating, and Projecting Your Value in Your Organization

> *"Thinking strategically is not for the faint of heart. It is about looking forward into the unknown."* —Rebecca Jones, Dysart & Jones

Description

Psychologists say that we are most likely to remember the first and last, so that is why we decided to make "Projecting Your Value" the last skill in our deck of 51. While all the skills in this book can be extremely valuable, we think that quantifying, demonstrating, and projecting your value in your organization may well be the most valuable skill you can learn. While this is such an important skill to master, sadly it is one that many librarians and information professionals lack.

Most everyone faces budget cuts, staff reductions, and layoffs at some time in their career, and many will experience this situation more than once. While budget cuts, layoffs, and even library closings are sometimes unavoidable, being able to quantify, demonstrate, and project your value within your organization consistently during good times can help you avoid becoming a casualty at a later time when economic problems abound.

Quantifying, demonstrating, and projecting your value must also go beyond the walls of your library. Many of our colleagues work in an environment where, at some level, they are reporting to someone outside the library. While most librarians understand and appreciate the value of their department to their organization, most people do not understand the critical role librarians and information professionals can bring to their organization. It is therefore our job to educate those people and teach them what we bring to the table and why the library is such an important and critical entity that it cannot be considered when the axe must fall.

So how do you quantify, demonstrate, and project your value to your organization? Well, one way is to be certain that your goals, objectives, and everything you are doing is contributing to helping your entire company or organization achieve its stated goals. This means knowing your organization's goals and objectives and making those goals and objectives the same ones for your library.

If your company goal is to increase sales, then you should be figuring out ways your library can help boost sales. Could that be achieved by:

- Providing a higher level of support to the sales force?
- Doing research on competitors that will help your company develop better products or simply know more about your competition's weaknesses that will help your sales and marketing staff produce better advertisements, collateral, or scripts for their sales calls?

Is your company looking at developing a new market for its products in China or Australia? If so, then you should be researching the conditions in those countries to provide vital information to those managers in the organization who are tasked with developing those new markets. And you should be doing this proactively. You should be meeting with those managers to find out what they need even before they ask for your help and support, because all too often, those managers don't realize what a vital role a librarian or information professional can play to help them be successful.

If you work in a nonprofit or government organization, are your organization's goals established to boost membership or to provide services to a specific number of people or other organizations? Whatever type or organization you work in, you should know your organizational goals by heart.

Knowing your organization's goals, being proactive, and taking the initiative to meet with your managers regularly and find out what they need before they go elsewhere to get it can be the difference between having a job when budget cuts hit in hard economic times or being on the street knowing that those managers made a terrible decision by eliminating your library and your job.

This Skill in Action

In previous chapters, we discussed the great success of Leigh Montgomery and how she has been able thrive as a newspaper librarian when many of her colleagues have lost their jobs and so many newspaper libraries have closed during this dismal time for the newspaper industry.

So how has Leigh survived and thrived when so many of her colleagues have lost their jobs? Perhaps most importantly, Leigh sets her quarterly goals based on her manager's goals, so they are both working toward the same end. In this area, Leigh always sets improving revenue streams as a goal for her and her library, because this is what the *Christian Science Monitor* is most focused on as well.

Next, Leigh is proactive about taking steps and communicating and quantifying her achievements. Leigh never assumes that her managers know what she's accomplished. She takes nothing for granted. She consistently reminds them of her value and tries to provide examples of where a librarian has made a difference.

If you follow Leigh's example, to align your goals with your organizational goals, always be proactive, and consistently communicate with your management, you will be going a long way toward quantifying, demonstrating, and projecting your value within your organization and, more often than not, you and your library will be one of the last departments to feel the adverse effects of an economic downturn.

Further Reading

1. Lustberg, A. (2002). *How to sell yourself: Winning techniques for selling yourself -- your ideas -- your message.* Franklin Lakes, NJ: Career Press.
2. Dysart, J. I. (2005). Why libraries fail & tips for staying alive. *Feliciter*, 3. Retrieved from http://www.dysartjones.com/presentations/feliciter_51_3_theme_feature_dysart.pdf
3. Germano, M. A. (2010). Narrative-based library marketing: Selling your library's value during tough economic times. *Bottom Line: Managing Library Finances*, 23(1), 5-17.

CHAPTER 10

Six Sure-Fire Strategies
for Acquiring and Developing New Skills

If you've reached this point in reading our book, chances are you may feel overwhelmed by how many possible skills there are to acquire or hone in order to advance or expand your career options. Hopefully, you are also eager to get out there to start acquiring those new skills you want to learn, but you may be wondering, "Well, how can I do that?" This chapter is devoted to sharing six tried and true methods for acquiring new skills in general, in addition to the "Tips to Acquire New Skills" section within the discussion of each skill presented in the book.

Strategy #1: Reading

In many of the tips sections of the discussion for each skill, we alluded to the number of books or articles that have been written about those skills. And at the end of each skill discussion, we've listed a few possible readings you might find helpful. Certainly, reading is a great way to learn about new skills and we highly recommend you do your own literature search to find books and articles that can help you learn more about those skills that interest you most. You might also want to explore the many websites we've listed or locate additional blogs and websites that contain pertinent information for the skills you want to master.

Strategy #2: Classes, Webinars, and Workshops

Taking classes or participating in webinars or in-person workshops can also be a very effective way to acquire new skills. Most library, information professional, or trade associations offer conferences and courses for professional development, and an increasing number of these courses and academic programs are being offered online.

These days, we also see many webinars or online chat sessions being offered for free. Don't overlook the free webinars or lunch meetings offered by vendors in the library and information world. Although these webinars are generally meant to acquire new customers, some also offer webinars or sponsor in-person meetings to discuss some of the hottest issues in our profession.

Even if a vendor webinar or luncheon is strictly a sales pitch, learning about a new product or service that you don't currently use or access could familiarize you enough with that product to be able to know what a potential employer is talking about if that product name is mentioned in a job description or an interview.

Additionally, a vendor-sponsored gathering is also a potential networking opportunity.

Strategy #3: Writing and Blogging

Another way of acquiring new skills or becoming an expert in different subjects is by writing or blogging, particularly in today's high-tech world where anything you write could be read by a very large audience.

Editors of publications in the library and information world are always looking for more content, especially if you're willing to write for free. But don't overlook this golden opportunity. People who start out as unknowns often develop a following when they publish their thoughts, ideas, research, etc., in trade publications or on blogs, listservs, websites, and social networking sites.

Writing about a particular topic helps you organize your thoughts and hone your insights on a particular subject. Additionally, whether it's justified or not, people assume that someone writing something to be read by the public has a certain level of credibility, and the more people who read your articles or postings, the more likely you are to be seen as an expert in that field.

Even if you don't feel comfortable writing articles or blogging, we encourage you to post a response to someone else's article or blog or comment on a listserv or Linkedin group. The more you contribute to any public forum, the more likely you are to gain recognition and credibility as an expert on a particular subject or for a specific skill.

Strategy #4: Networking

"Networking." Ah, there's that word again — an extremely important word when we talk about acquiring new skills, as well as being a skill in its own right. We covered networking adequately in "Social Networking" (Skill #14) and "Networking" (Skill #41), so there's no need to rehash that again. Suffice it to say that networking with the right contacts can help you acquire an expertise with just about any skill that is important to you.

Strategy #5: Mentoring

Mentoring is a topic we haven't covered yet in this book, but acquiring or being a mentor are strategies that can also help you learn new skills. Like any networking contact, a mentor with a specific expertise can help teach you a new skill you'd like to learn. On the flip side,  being a mentor can help you practice or hone a particular skill you'd like to develop. Finding or being a mentor can be as easy as asking. Some professional associations have formalized mentoring programs you can join.

Strategy #6: Volunteering and Mid-Career Internships

Volunteering and internships are two of the best and most often overlooked ways to quickly and easily acquire new skills and gain practical experience without incurring any expense. In "Volunteer Recruiting and Management" (Skill #25), we talked about hiring and managing volunteers and interns. Here we examine the flip side: how to acquire new skills by volunteering or being an intern yourself.

Many job seekers complain that employers are looking for someone who has a certain type of experience they are lacking. But how can you gain that experience if no one will hire you? Volunteering and internships are ways to break that paradoxical cycle.

By volunteering, you can acquire new skills and practical experience you cannot get elsewhere. Volunteering can also fill in gaps in your resume when you are between jobs.

In David's local History Room, volunteers are learning how to digitize, catalog, index, build new databases, and many other in-demand skills. Many of David's volunteers have gone on to find great jobs utilizing the skills they learned as a volunteer in the History Room.

When acquiring a new skill, it doesn't really matter whether you acquired it in a paid job or by volunteering. When your resume says you've had experience working on a live digitization project in the real world and you can show an employer the database you created on a website, it doesn't much matter if you were paid to build that database or not. The fact is that you had that real-world experience and you can perform the same task again for another employer without training. This breaks the cycle of no experience, no job.

Finding a volunteer opportunity is easy. Many organizations with limited hiring budgets are more than happy to take on volunteers and many cities and communities have websites where organizations can post volunteer opportunities.

Even for those with time constraints, volunteering is ideal, as many organizations can work around a volunteer's schedule. As previously mentioned in Skill #25, David has some volunteers who work as much as 20 hours per week and others that work just 2 hours per month. Even if you work full time, you can volunteer at many organizations during the evening or weekend, and an increasing number of organizations are looking for virtual volunteers who can work from home.

In addition to volunteers from outside the library world, David has many student interns in his local History Room, and an increasing number of mid-career interns who are unemployed or underemployed librarians. Intending to move on from their current jobs, there are also many practicing librarians who are seeking to learn new skills that they can't learn in their present positions. Even if you are a highly experienced, practicing librarian and you'd like to learn a new skill without going back to school, you can likely find a mid-career internship that would give you that opportunity without incurring any cost or interfering with your current job.

CONCLUSION

How to Create Your Plan
for Acquiring and Developing New Skills

Now it's time to determine which new skills you want to acquire or which skills you already possess need to be honed or improved.

How can you determine which skills you need for career advancement? You need to take an inventory of which skills you already have and your current level of expertise for them. Then review job ads that interest you and look at the skills they are asking for and the level of skill they are seeking.

Once you have decided which skills you need to acquire, improve, or hone, you need to decide what level of skill will best meet your needs. You don't have to become an expert at every skill. In many cases, you just need a basic familiarity with a particular skill.

How to Become an Expert: A Roadmap

At litemind.com/expert-roadmap, you'll find an interesting way to look at the process involved in moving from novice to expert. This article really speaks to the need to acquire new skills or improve your existing skills to give you more and better career options, and it defines five levels of expertise ranging from novice to expert.

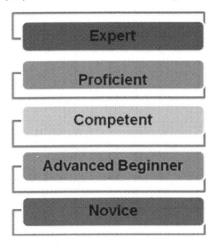

As you acquire new skills or improve and enhance your existing skills, you can see your progress at each level. As we progress along the skill ladder, our cognitive process changes at each stage on the continuum of skill development.

How will you know when you've become an expert with a specific skill? A novice may be characterized as one who is simply accomplishing a task. Novices:

- Focus solely on their first successes
- Generally don't take responsibility for their actions
- Are just following orders
- Are adhering to the rules
- Generally need to be closely monitored

In contrast, experts are intuitive. Experts can solve problems without prescribed rules. Practitioners can identify and describe a problem, but it often takes an expert to solve that problem.

It takes lots of practice and experience to become an expert. Because experts work intuitively, they may not even be able to articulate how they solve a problem, but they just know what to do.

Skills I Want to Acquire: My Personal Plan

We've talked a lot about the importance of acquiring new skills or bolstering skills you already may have. Now it's time for you to start working on your personal plan.

Create a list of skills, such as the ones below, that are most essential to you and the level of skill expertise needed. Do you want to be an apprentice, competent, or an expert in a particular skill? You can also list skills you have no interest in, but don't assign too many skills to this category. Be sure to create a plan for each skill you wish to learn or expand upon so that you have concrete steps and a date to reach your goals.

Skill/Level	Apprentice	Competent	Expert	N/A
Digitization				
Electronic Indexing				
ECM				
Archiving/RM				
Managing Digital Assets				
Website Design				
Web 2.0/Social Networking				

Skill/Level	Strategy for Acquiring Each Skill	Target Date
Digitization		
Electronic Indexing		
ECM		
Archiving/RM		
Managing Digital Assets		
Website Design		
Web 2.0/Social Networking		

It's important to remember that you don't need to be at the expert level for every possible skill. For example, for David's current job he doesn't need to be an expert in website design because there is a web designer on staff.

Still, David needs to learn enough about web design to be able to talk intelligently with the web designer. David must be able to express what he wants the website to look like in a way that the web designer will understand in order to implement David's recommendations. So for web design, David may only want to reach the "competent" level, but he certainly doesn't want or need to be an expert.

While David may consider himself at the "apprentice" level for website design, he might want to rise to the expert level if he is considering a new job where he would be much more involved in website design or if the web designer left the library and was not replaced due to budget constraints.

Keep your list handy and revisit it on a regular basis. If you continue to use and revise it as needed, you will be well on your way to new skills that will open new career opportunities for you.

Bibliography

Chapter 3: Introducing the 51 Hottest Skills for Librarians and Information Professionals

Colvin, G. (2009). Education for changing roles. *Information Outlook*, 3(7), 21.

Chapter 4: Computer/Technical Skills

2012 State of America's Libraries Report. American Libraries, 34. Retrieved from http://www.ala.org/news/state-americas-libraries-report-2013

Cameron, S. A. (2011). *Enterprise content management: A business and technical guide*. British Swindon, UK: Informatics Society Ltd. Retrieved from http://www.bcs.org/upload/pdf/enterprise-content-management.pdf

Dalkir, K. *Knowledge management in theory and practice* (2nd ed.). Cambridge, MA: MIT Press.

Fong, C. (2012). From manual to online cataloging. Retrieved from http://www.aallnet.org/main-menu/Publications/aall-ilta-white-paper/cataloging.pdf

Gilliland, A. J. (2008). Setting the stage. In M. Baca (Ed.), *Introduction to metadata* (1). Los Angeles, CA: Getty Research Institute. Retrieved from http://www.getty.edu/research/publications/electronic_publications/intrometadata/

McCraw, E. (2008). Libraries and digitization: The state we're in. Retrieved from http://www.elizabethmccraw.com/projects.html

Morris, S. L. & Rose, S. K. (2010). Invisible hands: Recognizing archivist' work to make records accessible. In A. E. Ramsey, W. B. Sharer, B. L'Eplattenier & L. Mastrangelo (Eds.),*Working in the Archives: Practical research methods for rhetoric and composition* (66). Southern Illinois University Board of Trustees.

St. Clair, G. (2003). Towards world-class knowledge services: Emerging trends in specialized research libraries part two: The customer perspective. *Information Outlook*. 7(6).

Chapter 5: Beyond Reference Skills

Bates, M. E. (2011). Why insight matters. EContent. Retrieved from http://www.econtentmag.com/Articles/Column/Info-Pro/Why-Insight-Matters-75773.htm

Evans, M. Excellence in financial management course 12: Competitive intelligence. Retrieved from http://www.exinfm.com/training/course12-1.doc

Nicholson, S. & Stanton, J. (2003). Gaining strategic advantage through bibliomining: Data mining for management decisions in corporate, special, digital, and traditional libraries. In H. Nemati & C. Barko (Eds.), *Organizational data mining: Leveraging enterprise data resources for optimal performance* (247-262). Hershey, PA: Idea Group Publishing.

Phelps, M. (2011). Know before you grow: Key resources for learning about your customers and competitors. Retrieved from http://www.huffingtonpost.com/marcy-phelps/know-before-you-grow-key-_b_922816.html?

Phelps. M. (2013). Ask the right questions to get the right answers: Effective market research requires preparation. Retrieved from http://www.cobizmag.com/articles/ask-the-right-questions-to-get-the-right-answers?

Chapter 6: Business and Management Skills

Bates, M. E. (2011). Think strategically: Add value to your business. *Bulletin*, 37(3), 43-45.

Kinkus, J. (2007). Project management skills: A literature review and content analysis of librarian position announcements. *College & Research Libraries*, 68(4), 352.

Mid-Hudson Library System. (2005). *Across the Board*, Summer, 2.

Schachter, D. (2008). Information pro as storyteller for staff, patrons, management. *Information Outlook*, 12(2), 28-29.

Chapter 7: Interpersonal Skills

Baldwin, M. (2011). Marketing & presentation. Retrieved from http://futureready365.sla.org/12/12/marketing-presentation/

Montgomery, L. Reach your maximum career potential workshop and webinar.

Hamlin, S. (2006). *How to talk so people listen: Connecting in today's workplace*. New York, NY: HarperCollins.

Chapter 8: Attitude Skills

Scott, P. (2009). Promoting your professional development: The value of being proactive. *Info Career Trends*.

Chapter 9: Intangible Skills

Bates, M. E. (2009). Do I look like a librarian? *Online*, (33)5, 64.

ABOUT THE AUTHORS

Deborah Hunt, MLS, ECMp

Deb Hunt is Library Director at the Mechanics' Institute (milibrary.org), a vibrant intellectual and cultural center serving the entire San Francisco Bay Area. The Institute serves its members with a large general-interest circulating and research library, the oldest chess club in the United States, and an active program of literary and cultural events.

Deb is Principal of Information Edge (information-edge.com), which specializes in enterprise, document and digital asset management, knowledge services, research and analysis, and library design and automation. In addition to her MLS, Deb is a certified Enterprise Content Management Practitioner and believes that learning never stops.

Deb is the 2013 SLA president and her presidency theme is "Transform Knowledge and Expertise into Strategic Value." She served as a director on the SLA board from 2008-2010. She is also an active member in the Association of Independent Information Professionals (AIIP) and served on the board of directors from 2001-2003. Deb is an award-winning part-time adjunct faculty in the Library Technology program at Diablo Valley College and has also taught for the League of Women Voters, InfoPeople, and UC Berkeley Extension. She is a frequent presenter at SLA conferences, Internet Librarian, and other venues for information professionals. Deb received her MLS from UC Berkeley and has moved forward from there, always leaping off the edge into the next opportunity to leverage and expand on her skills.

David Grossman, MLS, MBA

David serves as History Room and reference librarian for the Mill Valley Public Library (California), where he is currently constructing a digital archive with a workforce of 35 volunteers. David has more than four decades of experience in a variety of traditional and nontraditional library and information professional roles. Most of his career has been spent building, managing, marketing, and selling online systems and databases for publishers, airlines, and other businesses.

David has often been tapped as a motivational speaker on alternative career opportunities for librarians. David is also a part-time journalist in the airline/travel industry and previously authored a column on business travel for USAToday.com as well as a column called "What's Next" for Searcher magazine. His articles have also appeared in the Boston Herald, ABC News.com, and the print edition of USA Today. David holds a BA degree in Journalism, an MLS from the University of Michigan, and an MBA from the Kellogg Graduate School of Management at Northwestern University.

Made in the USA
Columbia, SC
16 September 2020